W9-BNQ-213

A Farm Country Christmas

A Treasury of Heartwarming
Holiday Memories

With best Christmas Wishes

Amy Rost-Holtz, Editor

With writings from Justin Isherwood, Edna Lewis, Dee
Hardie, Rachel Peden, L. M. Montgomery, Garrison Keillor,
Paul Engle, Laura Ingalls Wilder, Ben Logan, Bob Artley,
Robert P. T. Coffin and more.

Voyageur Press

A TOWN SQUARE BOOK

Edited by Amy Rost-Holtz
Designed by Andrea Rud
Printed in Hong Kong

99   00   01   02   03   5   4   3   2

Library of Congress Cataloging-in-Publication Data
A farm country Christmas : a treasury of heartwarming holiday memories / Amy Rost-Holtz, editor.
    p.   cm.
  "A Town Square book."
  ISBN 0-89658-440-2
  1. Christmas—United States—Literary collections. 2. Farm life—American. 4. American literature.
  I. Rost-Holtz, Amy 1970–
  PS509.C56F37   1999
  810.8'0334—dc21   99-20116
                                            CIP

Published by Voyageur Press, Inc.
123 North Second Street, P.O. Box 338, Stillwater, MN 55082 U.S.A.
651-430-2210, fax 651-430-2211

Educators, fundraisers, premium and gift buyers, publicists, and marketing managers: Looking for creative products and new sales ideas? Voyageur Press books are available at special discounts when purchased in quantities, and special editions can be created to your specifications. For details contact the marketing department at 800-888-9653.

An advantageous time
Page 1: *Fortunately for farm families, Christmas comes at an advantageous time of the year—after the rush of the autumn harvest but before the bustle of spring planting. (Photograph © Keith Baum)*

Silent night
Pages 2–3: *Christmas lights illuminate a New Hampshire village. (Photograph © William Johnson)*

Christmas wishes
Page 3, inset: *A turn-of-the-century postcard depicts a serene pastoral scene while bringing holiday good wishes.*

Tree trimmings
Facing page: *You're never too young to help put decorations on the family's Christmas tree. (Photograph © J. C. Allen & Son)*

Acknowledgments

Books are never created in a vacuum, and this book is no exception. Many people helped me put this volume together, and I would like to acknowledge their contributions here. Thank you to:

Bob Becker; June Coffin; Sally Cohen at Marian Dingham Hebb; Hualing Engle; Sean Ferrell at Macintosh & Otis; Sonja Hillgren, editor at *Farm Journal*; Marcia Kear at Frances Collin; Patricia Penton Leimbach; David McDonald and Ruth McDonald of the estate of L. M. Montgomery; Virginia McKay; Jeff Moen at University of Minnesota Press; and Beverly Shaver for granting permission to include text selections in the book.

To Gil Peterson, principal of Robert P. T. Coffin Memorial Elementary School in Brunswick, Maine, and Philip Dionne, who aided in the search for the estate holders of Robert P. T. Coffin.

To photographers J. C. Allen, Keith Baum, Roy Corral, Daniel Dempster, Bob Firth, William Johnson, Gary Alan Nelson, Leslie M. Newman, Paul Rezendes, Leonard Lee Rue III, Scott T. Smith, Lynn Stone, Stephen R. Swinburne, Ronald Wilson, and Marilyn "Angel" Wynn, for contributing their best work.

To Paul Wheeler and Jacqueline Szabo at Applejack Licensing for working out the details surrounding the use of Bill Breedon's paintings.

To Bob Artley and Sandi Wickersham, who kindly allowed their own artwork to be included in the book.

I also extend my appreciation to Michael Dregni, editorial director at Voyageur Press, for his guidance on this project.

Merry Christmas!
Amy Rost-Holtz

Curiosity
Above: *A curious cat investigates the barn's holiday wreath. (Photograph © Lynn Stone)*

Frozen farmstead
Facing page: *Winter may have frozen the fields, but it hasn't halted the rushing stream. A traditional red barn overlooks the scenic farmstead. (Photograph © Paul Rezendes)*

Landmarks
Page 8: *Quaint covered bridges are picturesque landmarks along a drive through farm country. The covering is certainly attractive, but it also serves to protect the roadway from snow and ice, which can easily build up on a river crossing. (Photograph © Keith Baum)*

Contents

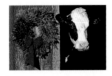

Introduction

*"When the snow piles up to the window sills and the promise is for more of the same—
for at least four more months—one needs not a little Christmas, but a great deal of it. . . ."*
—Virginia McKay, *Northern Delights*

What is so special about Christmas in farm country?

In farm country, sleigh bells are heard across the field. Families trek deep into the forests to cut their own Christmas trees and collect evergreen boughs for wreaths and garlands. Fathers spend long evening hours in lamp-lit barn workshops building toys for their children. Mothers bustle through warm kitchens, making homemade breads, cookies, and candy. Children carefully recite "And there were in the same country shepherds abiding in the fields . . ." in front of patient congregations of tiny churches.

Presents are opened on Christmas morning only after the cows are milked and the chickens are fed. The fruits of a year's worth of farm work are laid out on the dinner table for the Christmas Day feast.

And in the country, it is so quiet that you can almost hear the chime of each snowflake as it gently falls onto the fence surrounding the farm yard.

For many people, snowy hills, quiet churches, and snow-covered lanes are only pictures on Christmas cards. But for those who live the rural life, these scenes can be found just by stepping off the porch, on the walk between the house and the barn.

Festive Farmall
A 1965 International Harvester Farmall glows in the twilight of an Alaska dairy farm. (Photograph © Roy Corral)

A *Farm Country Christmas* is a collection of stories and essays celebrating these and all the other unique aspects of Christmas in the country.

Some of this book's selections, such as those by Ben Logan, Shirley Schoonover, Edna Lewis, and Bob Artley, are included because they trigger Christmas memories, sparking exclamations such as "That was what we did when I was growing up!" "Yes! That was exactly how it was!" or "That reminds me of the time when . . . ." Other writings, like those of Dee Hardie, Peter McArthur, and Paul Engle, inspire secret thoughts of "This is how a Christmas should be."

Some stories shine because of the eloquence of their authors—the essay of Robert P. T. Coffin is the gem that comes to mind here. Garrison Keillor's "Christmas Exiles" brings smiles with its recognizable characters and subtle observations of human nature.

The contributions of Laura Ingalls Wilder and L. M. Montgomery are excerpted from beloved childhood books; these stories are included not only because of nostalgia but also so that more children may discover them.

Finally, some stories strike just the right note in the heart and sum up the spirit of Christmas in the country, as the works of Dan Jorgensen, Bob Becker, and Justin Isherwood do.

All of the stories and their writers add a colorful piece to the patchwork quilt of memories and images that make up a farm country Christmas. In the process, they pay homage not only to the holiday but also to the natural, wholesome, hard-working lifestyle that is farm living. They capture exactly what makes Christmas in farm country special.

Fence rows
Hewn-wood fence rows line the road leading home to this country farmstead. (Photograph © Paul Rezendes)

Chapter 1

Christmas in Farm Country

"Those of us who have had the experience of driving to church in the dark on Christmas morn in a sleigh somehow never forget it, especially on those quiet winter nights when the stars seem to be so close to the earth, and is there a night when they seem closer than on Christmas?"
—Father Vernon J. Schaefer, *We Ate Gooseberries: Growing Up on a Minnesota Farm During the Depression*

Maybe it is because nature is quiet, snuggled under its blanket of snow. Maybe it is because the music is supplied by wind and branches. Maybe it is because the twinkling lights are the stars themselves. Whatever the reason, Christmas in farm country seems to have a beauty, a sparkle, a peace that cannot be found in a city.

Maybe it is because the farm fields are at rest. Maybe it is because their decorations are right outside the door. Maybe it is because this holiday was born in a stable. Whatever the reason, farmers and country dwellers seem to be on more intimate terms with Christmas than the rest of the world.

What distinguishes a Christmas in farm country from a Christmas elsewhere? Two writers—both, coincidentally, from Wisconsin—offer their answers in the following selections.

Twilight glow
Artist Bill Breedon captures the beauty and romance of a country borough at dusk in his watercolor painting "Twilight Glow." The residents of his quaint town revel in the snowy season with sleigh rides, snowball fights, ice skating, and sledding. (Artwork © 1999 Bill Breedon/Applejack Licensing)

Township Christmas

By Justin Isherwood

Christmas is a farmer's holiday," says writer Justin Isherwood. He should know, for he is not only an award-winning novelist and essayist but a farmer as well. He lives the farming life in Plover Township in north-central Wisconsin, and the title of his most recent book, *Book of Plough: Essays on the Virtue of Farm, Family & the Rural Life* (1996), clearly conveys how he feels about his chosen livelihood.

Isherwood's eloquent observations of country life and its details have appeared in *Audubon*, *Harrowsmith Country Life*, the *Wall Street Journal*, and in newspapers throughout Wisconsin. He is also the author of the novel *The Farm West of Mars* (1988).

The following Isherwood essay was first published in 1985 as part of *Christmas: The Annual of Christmas Literature and Art*.

Morning in New England
A Vermont township wakes to clear sky and a blanket of fresh snow. (Photograph © William Johnson)

WINTER BRINGS AN armistice to the countryside. The fields lie frozen, resting from the marathon event of summer just run with the sun. A peaceful product grows now from the land.

Christmas is a farmer's holiday. The reason is one of logistics. Memorial Day, Fourth of July, Labor Day all come in the green season, at a time when farmers cannot take liberties with their vocation. That the nation does celebrate with mass exodus all the cars packed and outward-bound to some haven, makes little difference.

Christmas comes at a time when work has cooled its fevered pace; the mows, granaries, and warehouses attest to the fulfillment of spring, summer, and harvest. The great work is finished.

Christmas has a primitive heritage. Sky watchers, who by nature were farmers, have for millenia noted the autumnal declination of the sun, noted the days becoming both shorter and colder. Because they had a direct relationship with the earth, this no doubt caused a reverberate fear the sun would sink altogether beneath the horizon, never to rise again.

Perhaps their celestial instrument was a tree seen from their habitation, perhaps a large rock. One day, two-thirds of the way through December, notice was given the sun would rise high again. This observation of the sun rising on the north side of the tree assured the farmer of the return of the sun and its connected growing season.

Modern farmers are yet tied to such ancient solar rites; some small muscle twitches at solstice. A near universal time of celebration, feast days, dances, and gift giving, its importance is held within our blood as an almost genetic response to a tilted planet's return swing about a nearby star.

Winter always provokes the struggle to survive. We have little difficulty in understanding why this is so, with blizzards and the worst cold yet to be told. The fall rush of canning, pickling, and hunting is but preparation to endure winter's coming, to survive to a distant spring.

Christmas is a time that makes us believers in magic. We as a people are so touched by the season that the selfish find themselves generous and the quiet find themselves singing.

It is a time when people become a little crazy, a time when normal people take to hiding things in secret places. It is a time when country children sneak to the barn on Christmas Eve to wait in the dark so that they might hear cows speak in human tongues.

It is a time when the weed pullers of summer walk their fields spreading thistle, sunflower, and rye seeds to gain the blessed flight of birds over their land, in belief that feathered prayers are best.

That the season is generous cannot be doubted. Cash register carols ring in the ears of the nation's GNP. While we have gained with invention a multitude of curiosities, we have lost something of self-expression, a quality thought quaint. Yet, it is personal expression that reinforces the bonds of friends and family and that repairs the rents made in the communal fabric. Its quality is one of goodness. For those having a generous solid character; what is put in will also flow out. Gifts make people as sure as people make gifts.

Remembered are all the knitted socks, caps, and mittens that mothers forced habitually on children, despite their best efforts to lose, mutilate, or outgrow them. Somehow mothers embodied good health in their children by the sheer number of such articles they could produce.

Flannel pajamas and quilts stuffed with raw wool or old wedding suits gave warm comfort in wood-heated, sawdust-insulated houses, which held pitifully little heat by morning.

Indeed, there were store-bought BB guns and toy trains that puffed flour smoke. There were Raggedy Ann dolls, and bicycles, and light bulb ovens, and baseball bats, and Flexible Flyers, and ice skates and, and, and—and all so child necessary. Beyond store-bought things were those contraptions, those inventions of glue and jack plane, alchemies of countersunk screw and dovetail mortise. They were gifts of the sort remembered, which gave off an affection if only from the lingering warmth of their manufacture. The spokeshave conveyed the heat of the builder into the wood grain. It was caught there, enmeshed in the fiber and net of a tree's core, only to be released slowly, the effect left to ripple across generations. There were dollhouses with tiny doors and itsy-bitsy cupboards. There were bookshelves and basswood mixing spoons, breadboards and spice racks. A coffee table with purple blemishes testified to the fence staples some great grandfather had driven into the tree, the iron taken till all that remained was the tinted tattle of wood. There was a child's wagon with lathe-turned white ash wheels. The basement oozed to the rest of the house the aroma of woodworking king. A cradle with

Stringing popcorn

After a day filled with sledding, snow forts, and snowmen, these farm children happily settle in for an evening of popcorn stringing. Most of the popcorn will become tree garland, but there is still enough for snacking. (Photograph © J. C. Allen & Son)

All is calm, all is bright
The chill of a winter morning is broken by a fiery sunrise over a Massachusetts farmstead. (Photograph © Paul Rezendes)

"Fordsicle"
A 1952 Ford 8N hibernates in the farm yard. (Photograph © Paul Rezendes)

birch headboard and rockers cut from wind-shaped limbs, a dulcimer of prized black walnut, a four-horse team with bobsled whittled from a block of white pine all took form there. Patient fingers made little ears and whittled almost breathing nostrils. The leather harness had all the lines; and the ironbound bobs were connected beneath by tiny iron rods so the bobs would swing opposite, just like the real bobsleds that hauled away the great trees of the once near wilderness. A gift of the early days, it ties together all the years. And a rocking chair—made from homegrown pine, pegged, and glued—lulled to sleep three generations of babies and rocked away the anxious days of two world wars and one jungle fight.

There were simpler gifts of a pancake breakfast taken to neighbors, or the sudden appearance of two full cords of oak firewood, or snowtires mysteriously installed. Notes found in the bottom of stockings promised two Sunday afternoons of ice-skating adventures or three Saturday mornings without chores to go romp the woods. Other simple notes promised to show a favorite fishing hole or a tree where flickers nested.

There was gift in all the cookies made and cut in the shape of angels, stars, and deer that flew. A haunting gift of powerful pride was given children, that they

might decorate stars from the humble perch of a country kitchen, cloistered behind its steamed-up windows.

The season was popcorn, grown in the garden and wildly crossed with Indian corn to produce among the bright yellow kernels spotted ones of red and purple. Shelled on the living room floor, the cobs were tossed to the fire. Hazelnuts were just for kids sitting cross-legged to crack. Ice skating on the irrigation pit meant popple branch hockey sticks and granite stone pucks. Hot cider, suet pudding, black fudge, cranberry bread, popcorn balls, and oyster suppers punctuated the season.

And the great green tree brought home from the woodlot in the emptied honey wagon swelled the whole house with its vapors. Its fragrance and good cheer left few lives untouched.

Christmas in the township catches hold of the generosity first given by the land. It is a season that knows what a good gift is, one that keeps on giving, echoing down what hard walls time makes. It was in just such a country place that angels were heard to sing of a child lain in a feedbox. It was, as all farmers know, a good place to be born and a good place for a promise to begin.

The Spirit of Christmas

By Bob Becker

In the hustle and bustle of the holiday season, the spirit of Christmas can easily be lost amid a flurry of ribbons, wrapping paper, cards, cookies, and parties. Fortunately, that spirit can be found again by taking a quiet winter walk through the countryside, with writer Bob Becker as a companion guide.

Becker is the descendant of German farmers and storytellers. Writing is his second career, the first ending with his retirement from the Wisconsin Department of Natural Resources in 1986, after thirty-two years of service. In his weekly newspaper column "Boot Prints," he spins yarns of his hunting and fishing adventures, shares memories of his boyhood on a Wisconsin farm in the 1930s, and profiles other folks with interesting stories to tell. He lives in the northern Wisconsin hamlet of Spooner.

The following selection appeared in Becker's column in 1994 and is included in a self-published collection of his writings entitled *Chips Off the Ol' Block!*

Spirited sled
Left in the snow long enough, even a sled will catch the Christmas spirit. (Photograph © William Johnson)

CHRISTMAS IS STILL a few days in the offing as I write. Around me, and elsewhere, the Christmas spirit burns warmly. Though Christmas will be past by the time these words appear, its spirit, I expect, will still be burning brightly.

I've been on a search these recent days, a quest of sorts, to find the spirit of Christmas. Christmas, after all, is more than a holiday on the calendar. Christmas has meaning and purpose, substance that adds value to our lives.

So I've been searching for the spirit of Christmas; quietly, casually, subtly, in my daily activities. I've looked and I've listened, hoping to savor such spirit wherever I could find it.

And indeed, find it I did.

There it was in a country church, for instance. It's a church I pass a hundred times a year. Lately, however, for some reason, it's taken on a different aura.

December 1911

A young girl wished her Ohio grandparents a merry Christmas and happy new year in 1911 with this golden greeting card.

There it stands, stately, dignified, on a snow-decked hilltop serene; the early morning sunlight reflecting from its stained-glass windows. Reaching for the heavens is a tall white steeple. And in that tower hangs an old bell, poised to peal its message across the countryside on Christmas day that the birthday of Christ is about to be celebrated.

There's perpetuity in that old church, I decide. Strength that seems to say that good will in mankind will prevail, even in our darkest hours.

Down the road a ways, a trout stream flows, its waters eddying black against the snow-covered marsh through which it passes. The scene is peaceful and tranquil. And in that peace and tranquility, I find too the spirit of Christmas. Peace on earth, after all, is a strong message of Christmas.

And then, one morning, while Harold Henriksen and I were moving out some Christmas trees out at the tree farm there on an old stone fence, three ruffed grouse sat perched, eyeing us as we went about our work. There they were, resplendent in their mottled gray-brown plumage, the morning sun shining on their speckled breasts.

There too, in those birds, I found a bit of the spirit of Christmas. For in them, and my pine trees into which they eventually flew, trees that I planted, I find love. Love for the land and the wondrous things it nourishes if given a chance. Love for the life it supports. Life upon which we mortals depend for our very sustenance.

I found the spirit of Christmas in people.

I found it in the excitement of our North Carolina gang as they announced over the phone that they'd be coming home for Christmas. And I found it in the voices of our Hayward gang as they described how they'd cut the family tree, then toasted hot dogs over a fire they built.

For in those things are joy, one of the prime ingredients of Christmas.

And I found it, in the warm gloves I received from the parents of a little girl, a youngster that I wanted to give a Christmas tree to, and did. It's in the exchange of gifts such as that, where the giving replenishes the giver, that the heart of Christmas lies.

Then, I found Christmas spirit in the dozens of small towns and villages, some barely cross-road hamlets, through which I passed. Where the symbols of Christmas hung from roadside poles and street lights. Long ropes of evergreen boughs, tinsel candy canes,

Snowy smiles
A pair of rosy-cheeked youngsters pauses after a whirl down a hillside. (Photograph © Stephen R. Swinburne)

red bells and silver stars, all intended to brighten the hearts of passer-bys.

Yes, I found the spirit of Christmas in many places. Some here, a little there. But nowhere in the totality like I did a recent day.

. . . There she was, dressed in a blue snowsuit, about eight years old I'd say. I saw her for some distance as I approached, about to pass by her country home with my load of Christmas trees. There she was, preparing to slide down a snowbank on her plastic toboggan sled.

And as I passed, she began to wave. Not just a weak little wave, but big happy waves with both hands, back and forth high above her head. Across her face spread a big happy smile.

There, I said to myself, is the spirit of Christmas that I've been looking for. There in that joyful, innocent, vibrant, sharing child was the true meaning of Christmas.

. . . After all, that's how it all had begun, I thought . . . with a child.

Morning light
Leaf Valley Church of rural Minnesota stands regal against the pale light of Christmas morning. (Photograph © Gary Alan Nelson)

Chapter 2

Traditions

*"The Christmas we used to have on Paradise Farm, when I was in
knee-pants and only knee-high to a grasshopper, had a lot to it. An
amazing lot. And the beauty of it was that about all the ingredients
that went into our Christmas were homemade. We raised
them all right there on the farm."*
—Robert P. T. Coffin, "Christmas on Paradise,"
from *Mainstays of Maine*

I n a literal sense, Christmas is no more than a date on the
calendar. It takes traditions—from meals to decorations to
activities—to transform the twenty-fifth day of December into
Christmas Day.

In the country, these traditions start with all-natural ingredients: evergreen boughs and trees collected from the woods,
fruits and vegetables picked earlier from the garden, chicken
and geese from the farmyard. When combined with family
rituals, such as caroling and putting up the tree, and the cus-
toms of the past—stockings filled with fruit, nuts, and candy
and sleigh rides through snowy hills—they form a delicious,
fragrant, lustrous holiday.

The following selections highlight some of the best Christmas traditions from farm country.

Deck the halls

*This cape-style house is all decked out in its Christmas regalia. For
some country folks, decorating their homes for Christmas is as much
fun as Christmas Day itself. (Photograph © William Johnson)*

The Taste of Country Christmas

By Edna Lewis

For Edna Lewis, memories are stored in recipes instead of scrapbooks. The smell of nuts, fruitcakes, baked ham, oyster stew, roast chicken, and fudge whisks her—and her readers—back to the Christmases of her childhood in Freetown, Virginia. Founded by former slaves, Freetown quickly grew into a true farming community, with every family and neighbor pitching in to help with farm events such as hog butchering, winter ice cutting, and holidays. Christmas was marked not only by feasts at home, but also the exchange of holiday food platters among neighbors.

Lewis's *The Taste of Country Cooking* is as much a memoir and tribute to Freetown as it is a cookbook. In the following excerpt, she shares her family's traditional Christmas menus and festivities.

Is it ready yet?
Grandma gives the turkey another baste under the hungry eye of her grandson. The farmhouse kitchen is the hub of farming activity throughout the year, but it really takes center stage at Christmas, when it yields a whole holiday's worth of baked goods and a bountiful Christmas Day feast. (Photograph © J. C. Allen & Son)

AROUND CHRISTMASTIME THE kitchens of Freetown would grow fragrant with the baking of cakes, fruit puddings, cookies, and candy. Exchanging gifts was not a custom at that time, but we did look forward to hanging our stockings from the mantel and finding them filled on Christmas morning with tasty "imported" nuts from Lahore's, our favorite hard candies with the cinnamon-flavored red eye, and oranges whose special Christmas aroma reached us at the top of the stairs. And for us four girls, there would also be little celluloid dolls with movable arms and legs that we so loved, and new paper dolls with their fascinating clip-on wardrobes. But mainly getting ready for Christmas meant preparing all kinds of delicious foods that we would enjoy with our families and friends during the days between Christmas Eve and New Year's Day.

There was a special excitement in the kitchens, as many of the things we prepared were foods we tasted only at Christmas. This was the only time in the year when we had oranges, almonds, Brazil nuts, and raisins that came in clusters. And although we were miles from the sea, at Christmas one of the treats we always looked forward to was oysters. The oysters were delivered to Lahore's in barrels on Christmas Eve day, and late on Christmas Eve we would climb the steps over the pasture fence and walk along the path through the woods to the store, carrying our covered tin pails. Mr. Jackson, the storekeeper, would fill some of our pails with oysters. And before we left he always filled our hands with nuts and candy.

We were excited by all the preparations for Christmas, but my own favorite chores were chopping the nuts and raisins for Mother and stirring the wonderful-smelling dark mixtures of fruits and brandy that would go into the fruitcake and plum pudding, and decorating the house with evergreens.

Just before Christmas a green lacy vine called running cedar appeared in the woods around Freetown and we would gather yards and yards of it. We draped everything in the house with it: windows, doors, even the large gilded frames that held the pictures of each of my aunts and uncles. We picked the prickly branches of a giant holly tree—the largest holly I've ever seen—which grew on the top of a nearby hill, and we cut armloads of pine boughs and juniper. My mother always gave the fireplace and hearth a fresh whitewashing the day before Christmas, and washed, starched, and ironed the white lace curtains. On

Christmas Eve my father would set up the tree in one corner of the room and we would decorate it with pink, white, and blue strings of popcorn that we had popped, dipped in colored sugar water, and carefully threaded. Small white candles nestled on tufts of cotton were the last decorations to be placed on the tree.

I loved the way the greens looked set off by the white hearth and walls and the stiff white curtains which they draped. In the evenings the soft orange glow from the fire and from the candlelight and the fragrance of the cedar and juniper mingling with the smell of chestnuts roasting always made me wish that Christmas week would last until spring, though I suspected that my mother did not share my wish.

The celebration of Christmas Day began before daybreak with the shooting off of Roman candles. With a great roaring noise they exploded into balls of red fire arcing into the still-dark sky. After they had all been set off, my father would light sparklers for us. We could never imagine Christmas without Roman candles and sparklers; for us it was the most important part of the whole day.

Finally we would go back into the warmth of the house for breakfast. There would be eggs and sausages and plates of hot biscuits with my mother's best preserves, and pan-fried oysters which would taste so sweet, crispy, and delicious. The familiar smell of hot coffee and cocoa mixed with the special aroma of bourbon, which was part of every holiday breakfast. We were allowed to smell, but never to taste this special drink of the menfolk.

We all dressed in our Sunday dresses for Christmas dinner. Dinner was at noon so that we would be finished in time for the men to feed the animals before dark. My mother would have been in the kitchen since five o'clock and half of the night as well, and when the dinner was ready we would gather round the table and sit for hours enjoying all the things she had prepared.

Christmas week was spent visiting back and forth, as at this time of year the men were able to take off some time. The women enjoyed tasting each other's baking and the men took pleasure in comparing the wines they had made at harvest time—wild plum, elderberry, dandelion, and grape. And they usually managed to enjoy a taste of that bourbon as well.

Every household had a sideboard or a food safe, and these would be laden throughout the week with all the foods that had been made for the holiday. Ours would hold baked ham, smothered rabbit, a pan of mixed small birds that had been trapped in the snow, braised guinea hen, liver pudding, and sometimes a roasted wild turkey that had grown up with our own flock (but usually a fat roast hen), and all the sweet and pungent pickles my mother had made from cucumbers and watermelon rind, crab apples and peaches. The open shelf of the sideboard would be lined with all the traditional holiday cakes: caramel and coconut layer cakes, pound cake, and my mother's rich, dark, flavorful fruitcake. There were plates of fudge and peanut brittle and crocks filled with crisp sugar cookies. The food safe was filled with mince pies, and fruit pies made with the canned fruit of summer.

Although there were no exceptions to our usual custom of sitting down together three times a day for meals, during Christmas week we were free to return to the food safe as many times a day as we liked and my mother would never say a word. But at the end of holiday week we were all given a home-brewed physic which was really vile! It was so vile I've never quite forgotten the taste of it.

On New Year's Day when all the Christmas decorations were taken down, we felt sad and let down; to us our house looked drab and naked, and although the visiting back and forth would continue until winter came to an end, Christmas was over.

Timeless tradition
Sugar dough, cookie cutters, rolling pins, frosting, and sprinkles—that is what Christmas traditions are made of. Baking and decorating—and eating—sugar cookies is an annual holiday event in many households. (Photograph © J. C. Allen & Son)

Christmas Eve Supper
Oyster Stew
Baked Country Ham
Scalloped Potatoes
Pan-Braised Spareribs
Crusty Yeast Bread—Ham Biscuits
Wild Blackberry Jelly—Watermelon-Rind Pickles
Yellow Vanilla Pound Cake—
Hickory Nut Cookies—Sugar Cookies
Dandelion Wine—Plum Wine
Coffee

A typical Christmas Eve supper would be very light for us children and nervously eaten because of our anxiousness to go to sleep and wake up very early to see what Santa had left in our stockings for us. We wouldn't eat much more than the oyster stew made from the first oysters of the season and crispy biscuits, but the grownups had a good time putting together special things and eating plentifully. . . .

Christmas Breakfast
Pan-Fried Oysters
Eggs Sunny-Side Up
Liver Pudding
Pork Sausage
Skillet-Fried Potatoes
Biscuits
Butter
Wild Strawberry Preserves
Bourbon
Coffee

Christmas breakfast was one to be remembered. While the activities of setting off the sparklers and Roman candles were going on, the house was filled with the aroma of frying oysters, coffee, and baking bread. A fine way to begin this special day.

Christmas Dinner
Roast Chicken with Dressing
Whipped White Potatoes
Baked Rabbit
Steamed Wild Watercress
Lima Beans in Cream
Spiced Seckel Pears
Sweet Cucumber Pickles
Grape Jelly
Biscuits
Hot Mince Pie
Persimmon Pudding with Clear Sauce
Fruitcake
Coconut Layer Cake
Caramel Fudge—Chocolate Fudge
Divinity Cream
Popcorn
Bowl of Oranges, Raisin Clusters, Brazil Nuts, Almonds
Blackberry Wine
Coffee

Christmas dinner was the more sober meal. A feast of winter harvest, it would consist of roast meat from hog butchering, a fat, old hen stuffed and roasted to a turn, rabbits and birds aged from hunting season, vegetables from summer canning, pickles, relishes, preserves, and jellies to go with the rich meat. There were pies, cakes, and puddings to last throughout the season. That was the time when the spirit of giving began. After dinner, platters of food began to be exchanged throughout Freetown. . . .

Bowl of Nuts and Oranges and Raisins
The bowl of oranges, nuts, and raisin clusters was Christmas. There was no other time of the year that the house had that particular aroma. It seemed as if the warmth of the hearth fire extracted the aromatic oils from the delicious Valencia oranges filling the house, mingling with the fragrance of pine needles, juniper berries, and holiday baking. We did enjoy the locally grown chestnuts, hazelnuts, and black walnuts, but the imported ones had more charm because they came only at Christmas from faraway Valencia, Jordan, and Brazil.

The bowl was set upon one end of the mantelpiece for all to see and enjoy. In the evening, while sitting before the fire, we would enjoy tasting the rich, meaty Brazil nuts that were bursting with oil when we chewed them. We were all fascinated with the crisp paper shells of Jordan almonds and their almost bittersweet flavor. There was nothing like the plump, chewy dried raisins, with a sweet flavor mingling with nuts—flavors we experienced only at Christmas. It is hard to describe the taste of those oranges; their sweetness had no equal as we ate them. Mother would gather up all the orange peels and dry them for flavoring sauces for summer puddings. She also used them to flavor tea. The fire would be snapping and crackling as if it, too, knew it was holiday time.

I can't remember Mother cautioning us not to overeat, but I do remember her telling us a story of a very hungry man who passed by a farmhouse while the farm wife was making pies and asked for one. She began to taste them to see which one was the best and ended up eating them all, whereupon she turned into a woodpecker. When you see a woodpecker, notice its front. That is the pie lady, still wearing her white apron.

Christmas feast
Left: *Every family has its own idea of how Christmas should taste. This Pennsylvania holiday meal features Dutch goose (a.k.a. pig stomach) as its centerpiece. (Photograph © Keith Baum)*

Sweet treats
Above and below: *Pies and candy are just a couple of the myriad treats that sweeten a holiday season. (Photograph, above © Ronald H. Wilson. Photograph, below © Keith Baum)*

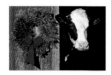

Christmas at Thornhill Farm

By Dee Hardie

In 1955, writer Dee Hardie and her husband Tom bought a rundown 1843 farmhouse outside Baltimore, Maryland. Christening the house and its accompanying acreage "Thornhill Farm," she transformed the boxy house into a warm, festive home for their young family. Through the decades, the history of her life and that of the Hardie family became intimately entwined with the history of that farm.

For years, she shared her life and experiences in a monthly column for *House Beautiful* magazine. The popularity of those columns prompted her to write *Hollyhocks, Lambs and Other Passions: A Memoir of Thornhill Farm* (1985), her chronicle of a farm life full of animals, flowers, friends, family, and traditions.

As far as Hardie is concerned, Christmas is the celebration of the year at Thornhill. As the following excerpts from *Hollyhocks, Lambs, and Other Passions* shows, the combination of the holiday and the natural resources of the farm bring out the artist in her. Although she admits that her decorating and other preparations are hard work, they are obviously a labor of love—love of natural beauty, a love of Christmas, and a love of traditions.

Brilliant entrance
A brilliant tree stands surrounded by classic Christmas toys in the entryway of an old Victorian home. (Photograph © Daniel Dempster)

. . . Tom says I celebrate Christmas all year round which is as exaggerated as Christmas sometimes is, but I must admit I do hoard throughout the year, often thinking, in the middle of June, that I've found the right present for the right person. It's my own little game, mix and match. I push these presents into a pine cupboard in our bedroom. Then in early December I have a marvelous time rediscovering my loot. Christmas is the one time of the year when I don't have to take down the props the very next day. There is a time for tinsel, and this is it.

Christmas, if you look at a calendar, happens all by itself, as do all the holidays, but Christmas, most of all, needs no invitation. Yet to celebrate, truly celebrate, takes time and care. I have one friend John who combs our woods at Thornhill for pine cones, then ties them with bright tassels to decorate gifts. A neighbor Jane makes a succulent pea soup, braids homemade bread, to serve on Christmas Eve when the carolers come by on horse. After those hearty bowls of soup, the carolers mount to go home, riding away with extra-tall flickering sparklers, saved from the Fourth of July, and given to them at the front door. It is quite a sight. . . .

Robert, another friend, always has an orange and onion salad because as a boy in France during the war there were no oranges. Except on Christmas morning. He thought then it was Père Noël's gift, but now he realizes they were harvested by clandestine methods, known only to mothers. Especially French ones. . . .

. . . I can't possibly imagine Christmas without a tree. They are our constant Christmas glow, our exclamation points throughout the house. And we usually have three.

Every year I forget how tired I was the year before. Every year I become a born-again Christmas addict. And by the second week in December our trees are dressed in glory. The tallest tree is in the living room, and at the top is a fine Woolworthian parrot. Now an ancient age twenty-five, the parrot was bought, jointly, by our children. It's one parrot that never talks back. And under the lowest bough of the tree is a collection of toys—the wooden horse our children once rode, a miniature Welsh dresser, *my* china doll from England, Fiona Barley. The tree itself is looped with golden beads, hung only with bright balls. We save the ornaments, ones we've made, been given, or gathered on trips, for the dining room tree. Each ornament has its own story, makes us remember.

The dining room tree must be plump as a goose, must reach at least to my nose. Sometimes I think if we could only have one tree I'd choose to put it in the dining room. It makes every meal an occasion; and eating dinner by the sparkle of a tree is magic. I first saw a dining tree in Finland, and the Finns, who have the darkest of winters, keep their trees up forever. Our dining room tree doesn't take itself quite as seriously as does the one in the living room. Perhaps because it's short and fat and fun.

Standing in the kitchen is the living tree, planted later in a border hedge around a field. This tree is decorated with sheep cookies Beth has made, tied on with thin red ribbons. She always makes extra cookies to give away to friends who come by during the holiday. Sometimes I box them as a present, other times we just give one or two as tree ornaments. It depends on how well the baking goes, how many bake into a tasty flock, how many we burn in the attempt. . . .

The kitchen tree is decorated as well with a bouquet of spiced pears, oranges, lemons, and limes, embroidered with designs of cloves. The scent is delicious. To make the job easier, I first make the holes in the fruit with an ice pick. I also make colonial kissing balls the same way. Using grapefruit, I ice-pick the holes, then completely cover the grapefruit with tiny sprigs of boxwood. Soon the grapefruit looks like a round green porcupine. After making a few, I hang them with broad red ribbons around the archways of the house.

In earlier years the children even put a tree in the barn for the sheep. Decorated with biscuits dipped in honey, it seemed appropriate, again going back to the manger. One year Tommy and I went to a tree farm to cut one down. Right next to us, doing the very same thing, was his idol, the great Orioles third baseman Brooks Robinson. We were so excited we left the saw

All natural

No plastic tinsel or aluminum trees here! In the country, the forest is still a plentiful source of natural Christmas decorations, such as evergreen boughs. (Photograph © Stephen R. Swinburne)

behind. And perhaps showing off near his hero, Tommy carried the cut tree by himself—absolutely upright. The way he carried the cross when he was an acolyte in church. A family went by and said, "I see a tree with legs," and we all laughed and it was fun, the way spirits should be around Christmas. Seeing Brooks Robinson, I'm sure, was Tommy's best Christmas present of all.

Another early gift for children is the felt Christmas calendar my friend Margaret makes. She used to pretend that her own children had made them, as she didn't think much of her own stitches, but these calendars are charming. The calendar is a square of bright yellow felt, twenty by thirty inches, with a large green Christmas tree sewn in the center. Along three sides, the left, lower, and right, she sews a row of small yellow pockets each numbered in green felt, from one through twenty-three, up until a red pocket heralds the twenty-fourth of December. In each pocket is a tiny token attached to a tiny safety pin—a star, a butterfly, a golden acorn, a bumblebee. Each day a pocket is opened, the present pinned onto the center Christmas tree. And each year she replenishes the pockets with new surprises.

I use ribbons more than felt, and in the yellow dining room I tie big red bows on the brass sconces. In the red library I hang floor-length streamers of green ribbons from the very top molding. But first I staple a three-inch ribbon with the Christmas cards we have received, each about five inches apart. Rather than sitting the cards in the bookcases or piling them in a bowl, I find these streamers and cards add a gaiety to the room. They greet friends almost immediately, and flutter when the front door opens. It's like a roomful of miniature pictures. I also sew silver Christmas balls to graduated lengths of red ribbon, then hang them in a Palladian curve over entrances of bedroom doors. Once I get started, I can't seem to stop.

Now that the children are grown, I seem to have more time. But it wasn't always like this. When our children were young, Christmas was another challenge of parenthood, like teaching them how to tie shoes. Would I, could I, ever get it all tied up and packaged by the big night? We overspent and underestimated our children's intelligence. And it was all so sadly calculated. If Todd gets eight presents and a train from Grandpa, what are Tommy's matching gifts? If Louise gets that doll, would Beth like a clown? And engi-

neers we certainly were not. Little red wagons always limped along on Christmas Day because we always lost that last little screw. And there was that jungle gym that never did get put together, just put away before the morning eyes of children ever saw it. We learned never to buy anything that had to be assembled.

What I assemble now are wreaths. And I wreathe everywhere—from making a Christmas collar for the larger-than-life-size goose decoy on our front lawn, to putting circles of green on the stable doors of friends. These wreaths can be made of any evergreen—fir, balsam, moss cypress—but I always use boxwood because it is mine. I like its dark green shiny glow and that some of the wreaths last for months. One Easter Tom asked me if I didn't think it was time to take the Christmas wreath from the inside of the kitchen door. It was still green although it was late April. Sometimes for a spring party I make another boxwood wreath, pinning yellow daffodils and white narcissus against the green. Any flower will brighten the garland, and a more delicate, lacy look, I discovered, was when I put white lilacs and apple blossoms on the boxwood wreath.

Our boxwood are always waiting for us, no matter what season. When we first planted these bushes some thirty years ago, they were knee-high greenery. Now they are five feet tall, wider than Santa Claus, and just as generous. When Agnes first insisted we plant them, I thought of them merely as fringe benefits, but now they are an important part of Thornhill traditions. And if a bush can be part of a family tree, I consider these boxwood bushes close relations, always ready to give when asked.

I prune them in early December for Christmas. I break the limbs from deep in the center of the bush with my hands, never with clippers. And I gather enough for wreaths and garlands. Then I pat the bushes and thank them for their winter kindness. The boughs always spring back, as if to say, "Okay, we've done our part, now it's up to you."

The first wreath is the most exciting. Christmas is almost here. That first wreath goes right on the inside of the kitchen door. The others I make live outdoors. And as I often give wreaths as presents, I make them whenever I find time—often under the dryer at the hairdresser's. They are that easy. I arrive at Mr. Ryan's hair salon, which is in a converted barn, with a basket full of boxwood, a straw wreath form, and lots of fern pins. Both the wreath forms and pins, which are like miniature croquet wickets, can be found at the five-and-ten, my source for all my decorating, or at any florist.

The wreath forms measure fifteen to eighteen inches in diameter, edge to edge. I place the wreath on the kitchen table, or my lap, and start pinning the branches of boxwood around the circle counterclockwise or clockwise. It all ends up the same. I overlap, slightly, every bough. This way each fern pin is covered-by the next fan of greenery. Then I pin the inner circle, and the last is the outer rim. To make a fuller, more complete wreath, I pin the backside as well.

Self-taught, I realize there must be a more proper procedure for making a wreath, careful steps to insure a perfect circle. And if any wreath of mine was ever

Colorful combinations
Both photos: *The natural ingredients of farm country living spark the creativity of those who live there. Holiday visitors to these Pennsylvania homes are greeted with colorful combinations of fruit, evergreen boughs, and other green leaves. (Photographs © Keith Baum)*

Going all out
An Indiana family goes all out when decorating their farmyard for the holidays. (Photograph © Daniel Dempster)

entered in a garden club competition, I'm sure I'd be disqualified immediately for errant fern pins sticking out from under the green. But there is no way that is any quicker. And that's the fun of it. I can whip up a wreath in twenty minutes. If a curve of the wreath seems to be a bit wild, a bough out of line, that simply adds to its natural charm.

Our own front door wreath and the wreaths I give away I decorate with small ornaments that can be used the next year on the Christmas tree. Or sometimes I decorate with fresh fruit. Over the years I've used green grapes and small Madonna apples, wooden toys, and old lace. Whatever takes my fancy. I fasten these ornaments with fern pins, or tie them with *very* narrow ribbon. The big bow is often of Scottish plaid or a deep red grosgrain ribbon. I hang these door wreaths with ribbon by looping it through the circle, then taking both ends and thumbtacking them high to the unseen top edge of the door frame. If I have time to make inside window wreaths for the red library, I leave those wreaths, solidly green, adding no additional color.

Our dining room table is the last scene to set. And again I often do it days ahead, much preferring to dress the table than the turkey. A great-grandmother's cloth, like Mrs. Cratchit's gown in *A Christmas Carol*, "twice-turned but brave with ribbons," covers the oval table. It is turkey red, and in the center I use a boxwood wreath as a green nest to cover a large patch of age. I fill the nest with golden balls sewn to tartan or red ribbons. The ribbons stream from the nest like a Christmas maypole and on each ribbon, written with glitter, is the name of a member of the family or a friend. These ribbons and balls become place cards as well as souvenirs of a Thornhill Christmas, our guests taking them home to put on their own tree. At each place at the table I also put a Christmas cracker, the kind you pull at a child's party, complete with paper hats—a tradition I borrowed from England. I like to think they fit the occasion. Christmas, after all, is our biggest birthday party of the year.

With the house decorated, food cooked ahead as much as possible, presents for my family that please me, I take off. I *never* go to the marketplace the week before Christmas. I find it helps my spirit, makes it easier to follow the star. Instead I go to the Baltimore Museum of Art to feast, to look once again at the French Impressionist paintings and the fine collection of American furniture. This solitary venture is a gift of time, a gift to myself. Then I go home and open a bottle of champagne with Tom. I like Christmas to bubble from the very beginning.

OH TANNENBAUM!

By Patricia Penton Leimbach

With a wry sense of humor and a keen eye for everyday details, Patricia Penton Leimbach has documented her forty-plus years of rural life in her weekly column "Country Wife," which appeared in the *Chronicle-Telegram* of Elyria, Ohio. Her works have been collected into three books, including *All My Meadows,* from which this selection was taken.

Leimbach lives with her husband Paul, a fourth-generation farmer, at End'O'Way, their farm in Vermillion, Ohio.

Of all the joys of rural living, one of the most exquisite is cutting your own Christmas tree . . ." or so it says here in *Reader's Digest*. The author didn't have to explain that she was a new arrival on the rural scene. Nobody who has lived in the country forever, who regularly tramps about a cold feedlot, carries heaters through snowdrifts to outlying barns, or bounces over frozen ruts after firewood with a tractor and wagon, describes the ordeal of struggling down to the pasture with a saw and an ax and dragging home a tree as an "exquisite joy."

Those are clearly romantic notions engendered by old Christmas card scenes, and the idealistic breed of back-to-the-landers swallow them hook, line, and sinker. Something tells me, too, that all those city papas coerced into driving twenty-five miles into the boondocks to a "cut it yourself" place would describe the whole ritual as something less than exquisite. Probably takes two bourbons to recover! Those guys aren't all that handy with an ax; and they soon discover that the trees in the meadow aren't any more perfect than the ones the Odd Fellows are selling on the corner.

This is not to imply that we farm folk think of our woods and fields and trees as ho-hum. On the contrary, Paul would cheerfully slaughter anybody who laid a hand on one of those white pines he planted over on the river bank. Cut them for Christmas trees? Never!

We do have native cedar trees aplenty, and many a lean year we were forced to settle for one of them. Nobody who knows cedar trees is going to describe them as exquisite on either end of the trek. Cedar trees in shelter belts have been a great boon to the American prairie, but blue spruce they are not! A cedar is a dark grayish-green blob of tree which grows lovelier as you recede from it. Up close it looks like a fugitive from a pulp mill. Each branch has tiny barbs which prickle and scratch and carry an odor reminiscent of dog urine. The only way to camouflage one is to spray it liberally with paint and pine oil. The price is right, but everything else is wrong.

Out front in the snow a spare Scotch pine leans against a bright red picnic table looking as much like a Christmas card as it's likely to look. Dad brought it home and the kids have registered their complaints.

"Scrawny-looking thing!"

"You call that a Christmas tree!"

"That's not tall enough!"

As far as I'm concerned, it's "exquisite." As for Paul, he too has a clear memory of what it was to trek to the pasture with an ax, bring home a cedar, and struggle to make something lovely of it.

No Christmas tree that ever came into the house was tall enough, short enough, full enough, shapely enough, or green enough to suit our kids. Nor did we ever decorate a tree with our accumulation of trinkets—ancient and new, made or remade, elegant or rinky-dink—that we didn't appraise finally as splendid.

The fact is that a Christmas tree, like the holiday itself, is pretty much what you make it.

Above: *A plump evergreen basks in the glow of the lamplight and the warmth of the hearth. (Photograph © Stephen R. Swinburne)*

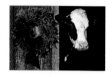

Homage to a Christmas Tree

By Rachel Peden

One of the most cherished Christmas traditions is bringing home a tree. However, finding just the right tree—one that fits the family as well as the living room—is often a challenge. In the end, it is sometimes the not-so-perfect pine tree that turns out to make the perfect Christmas tree, as newspaper columnist and farm wife Rachel Peden explains.

Born, raised, and schooled in Indiana, Peden married a Monroe County farmer. She shared the details of farm living with the both country and city readers of "The Almanac of Poor Richard's Wife" and "The Hoosier Farm Wife Says," columns she began writing for Indiana newspapers in 1946. These columns were the starting point for her 1961 book *Rural Free: A Farmwife's Almanac of Country Living.*

In this December entry from her almanac, Peden remembers one Virginia scrub pine that won not only a spot in her home but also in her heart.

Delegate, delegate, delegate
A good manager knows that she doesn't need to be tall to decorate the top branches—she just needs to hire someone who is. (Photograph © J. C. Allen & Son)

WE SET UP the Christmas tree yesterday—a five-year-old Virginia pine—and Carol decorated it as she wished.

When the children were little, we used to go on the tractor to Blaine's woods and cut a small cedar for our Christmas tree. When we brought it into the house, cold, sharp-needled, and usually with a bird's empty nest in it (because the children hunted until they found one that did have a nest), it gave the room a delightful cedary fragrance.

Now that the children are older their holiday activities extend in a wider range (such as the 4-H caroling party when the Maple Leaf club and sponsors go in Warren's truck to carol for the elderly and shut-in of the community as preliminary to a party). We buy a tree, although Dick has never really got reconciled to paying money for one.

We were driving along old Highway 37 yesterday afternoon when we saw the sign advertising Christmas trees, and a long row of them freshly cut and piled greenly on a grassy bank at the Lilly farm. They were seventy-five cents apiece, and Dick suggested it might be the place to get one.

We began the ordeal of making a choice. It is hard for Carol because she is hard to please—she would like to have a tree as tall as a giant redwood, she is critical of every branch and needle. For me the choice is hard for a different reason. It's like choosing one dog from a whole kennelful. Every one looks at me with pleading: "Love me, take me home." If I look at

more than three, I am lost. My way is to take the first one I touch. I picked up a tall one at the first of the line; the gummy juice from its trunk came out on my bare hand. "I like this one," I said.

"I don't," said Carol. "It's crooked. It's almost yellow."

But we took it anyway. I gave the tree seller seventy-five cents and he thanked me in a pleasant, Scotch-accented voice, adding: "And I hope you and yours have a good Christmas day."

Carol got into the back seat of the car, intending to sulk all the way home, but unfortunately for that plan the tree was so tall it had to have the whole back seat and both back windows had to be rolled down besides to make room for it, unbent. She had to sit in the front seat with us and soon forgot to sulk. When the pine was set up in the living room and decorated with colored lights, shining metal icicles, and the fragile Christmas-tree balls and birds that have shared many Christmases with us, it looked beautiful.

After it had stood in the warmed room a short time, it began to give off a delicate, flowerlike perfume. When in the evening the tree lights were turned on, warm against its long, paired needles, the fragrance deepened. This perfume, characteristic of Virginia scrub pine, was a delightful surprise from the Christmas tree.

This is the Christmas tree I shall remember longest. Its tiny cones are rough and turn backward against the sticky bark. It is tall and outreaching, dense enough to hold decorations and small gifts in its branches. The branches come out of the main trunk at intervals, in an arrangement of five branches not quite in a circle, and the smaller twigs come out of the branches in the same fineness, suggestive of the five points of a Christmas star. The Virginia scrub pine seems born to be a Christmas tree.

But there is another reason why my heart warms toward this fragrant, not ungainly, green tree. It will grow on abandoned or abused land, where other trees will not grow. At first only such plants as cat brier anti wild honeysuckle, which like a sterile and acid soil, will grow where Virginia scrub pine is. By the

"Happiness be yours"
A farmhouse and holly grace this embossed Christmas postcard from the early 1900s.

Rise and shine
Laden with country-style ornaments, ribbons, and candles, a country Christmas tree sparkles in the dawn. (Photograph ©
William Johnson)

time it is about five years old, it has made its own
seedlings, holding the precarious soil in place and
adding fertility until finally, after twenty-five or more
years, the spring-lovely redbud and dogwood appear
in the pine thicket. When many generations of Virginia pines have come and gone, the soil is fertile
enough to support other, better forest trees. In seventy-five years almost any forest tree or plant can sub-
sist on what the Virginia scrub pine has made possible.

Notes of a Christmas Tree Grower

By Beverly Shaver

There is one kind of farm where holiday preparations extend throughout all twelve months of the year: a Christmas tree farm. Operating such a farm may seem to be the ultimate marriage between the holiday and the farming life, but it makes for a busy December, as freelance writer Beverly Shaver can attest.

For many years, Shaver, a retired college professor, helped her daughter and son-in-law on their Christmas tree farm in northern California. Despite the frenzy of customers and tiring physical exertion, Shaver says that work on the farm was "a wonderful, bonding, enriching family enterprise each year." Her experience on that most Christmas of farms offers not only a unique perspective of the Christmas tree tradition, but it also provides insights into American lifestyles, family dynamics, and human nature.

The following story first appeared in the November/December 1993 issue of *Country Journal*.

Decisions, decisions. . .
A visitor to a Christmas tree farm evaluates the contestants for tree of the year. She is one of more than 33 million North Americans who celebrate the holiday with a real wood-and-needles tree. (Photograph © Keith Baum)

THERE ARE NO piped Christmas carols, no limp strings of multicolored light bulbs, and no wire fencing around the Christmas trees we have for sale. And they haven't spent any time leaning, flattened, against a wall. They stand waiting where they have grown, in the open fields, strongly rooted, sap high. For us they represent a heavy investment of emotional and sweat equity.

With the apples picked and the pumpkins departed with the ghosts and witches, our tranquil valley is on the cusp of winter. And now at Thanksgiving, the annual countdown begins. Like Sears, Macy's, and Woolworths, we must make our black-ink margin for the year during the next five weeks.

Feeling both eagerness and dread, we post our signs on the live oaks lining the road from Highway 1—La Pajarosa Christmas Trees. Choose and Cut. And in lowercase type, All One Price. (We have learned that uniform pricing eases the terrible problem of choice, and eliminates the bargaining in which we are always losers.) We avoid eye contact with passing neighbors who have not been happy about the odor of dried septic tank sludge, which we dump several times a year on the fields to energize the trees.

We take our saws to be sharpened by Mr. Higgins's cross-section files. He observes that we've lost two saws to last year's cutters and gives us a little sermon on the decline of morals as he works. We hang the honed blades in the shed, recalling uneasily some near disasters with flighty saw wielders and debate whether we should increase our liability coverage.

Soon exuberant carloads of dogs, children, and sneakered adults will invade the valley, stopping—despite the posted signs—to pound on doors for directions. Theirs is a race to be the first to choose a Christmas tree before "they're all picked over." Life at the farmhouse for five long weeks will be a blur of invasions and interrupted daily routines. Faces will appear at our bedroom windows at the unmercantile hour of 6:30 a.m. ("Thought I'd stop on the way to work.") Tree buyers will ask apologetically to borrow a tape measure in the middle of our dessert ("We're not sure the tree we like will clear the living room ceiling."), leave trails of caked mud across the hallway on their way to our bathroom with a child, and try to buy our pickup out from under us. Their manic dogs, like Fascist storm troopers, will shatter the peaceful world of our gentle Labrador retrievers.

But it is impossible to resent our customers. They come wearing their Christmas faces, in ragged family phalanxes, disarmingly festive. They are traditionalists in a ritual that dates to eighth-century Germany, where Saint Boniface sent his Christian converts into the snow-covered forest to find "a little fir tree, the sign of endless life for its branches are evergreen." Our tree seekers have childhood memories of the scent of piney pitch in a fresh-cut trunk, an abiding sense of the land, and a need to reconnect their Christmas symbols with old verities and authenticities. And every year they ensnare us willy-nilly in that warm tide of generosity, expectation, and celebration that characterizes the American Christmas.

What constitutes just the right tree becomes a lesson for us each year in psychology, sociology, and domestic relationships. Tolstoy's distinction between happy and unhappy families—the former resembling each other, the latter each being unhappy in its own way—is never more apparent than on a Christmas tree field. Sunny, closely knit families move into the fields in tight cadres like platoons on a combat mission. They decide quickly, pay happily, and drive away exuding satisfaction. Families in conflict scatter in lone search, shrilling at one another across the fields to "come see this one." The power struggle becomes high drama as they try to agree on criteria. And there are times when it seems some of the great battles of history have been fought in our fields.

We could tell market researchers a thing or two about market segmentation. Scotch pines, for example, are popular with the upscale corporate folk who spray them white like the *Nutcracker* trees and install them in cathedral-ceilinged living rooms. The plain-Jane Douglas firs, thin-needled and unassuming, are the People's tree, and they go off in station wagons and pickup trucks, while the smaller, chic incense cedars get hauled away in BMWs and Volvos to condominiums. The sturdy little Monterey pines that grow close to the parking area and have plenty of branch space for tinsel are favored by seniors. And our few Arizona cypresses, capriciously branched and nonconical, are snapped up by the arts-and-crafts folks, who plop them into buckets of water and cover them with tiny candles.

During the last few days of the season, the bargain hunters appear. They always say they couldn't get away from work earlier and then pretend they can't read the price in large print on the signs. They are uncritically ready to take whatever is left—at a drastically reduced price.

Fields of firs

A quick wagon ride takes visitors to the heart of the evergreen fields at Elizabeth Farms. The most popular choices for Christmas trees are the balsam fir, Douglas fir, Fraser fir, noble fir, Scotch pine, Virgina pine, and white pine, says the National Christmas Tree Association. (Photograph © Keith Baum)

And there are our regulars. The ebullient family with nine children that comes tumbling out of their ancient station wagon two days before Christmas Eve. They troop about, consulting explosively, then appear, shiny eyed, with *two* small trees. "There are so many of us, we put one in the parlor and the other in the verrry beeg kitchen!" We pocket their tightly wadded bills and help stuff the trees in among the densely packed small fry.

Then there is the woman who likes to dye her tree blue to match her couch. And the man in a Caterpillar tractor cap who, year after year, threatens to bring his power shovel, dig up an 8-foot blue spruce, and replant it in his front yard. And there is the couple who always offers a trade for a tree and, when turned down last year, left a litter of yelping pups in our toolshed anyway. There are the single parents with an 8- or 10-year-old who want a perfect miniature tree for a dollhouse. And the Filipinos who like to mail a 3-foot cypress to an elderly relative in Manila.

Enshrined in our hearts from last Christmas is the small fellow who hip-hopping behind his mother, was single-mindedly indifferent to all trees. Then, hitching up his drooping jeans, he came to us, carrying the saw carefully, blade outward as instructed. "Can we have that one?" he asked, pointing to a crackly dry, orange deodar cedar.

"You don't want that, it's dead, given up the ghost," we said.

"I *do* want it, we *do*, don't we, Ma," was the passionate response. And off they went with the moribund cedar, the boy crouched beside it while we shouted warnings about fire hazards.

At length the reindeer night approaches and commerce slows to a trickle. Our energies are depleted, our spirits a little numbed by the effort to respond to a stream of hopes and sighs, to expedite choice, to reassure, and to deal with tense moments, such as when two purchasers converge on the same tree simultaneously and one must be pacified with as near a

Sea of scarlet

Above: *Christmas tree farmers aren't the only ones who work all year for a holiday harvest. After a year's worth of tender care, the owners of this poinsettia farm are rewarded with a brilliant scarlet sea of petals, blooming just in time for the rush of holiday buyers. (Photograph © Keith Baum)*

Evergreens for everyone

Right: *Rows upon rows of evergreens welcome holiday visitors to Elizabeth Farms in Brickerville, Pennsylvania, one of about 15,000 Christmas tree farms in North America. According to the National Christmas Tree Association, Christmas trees are grown in all fifty United States, with Oregon, Michigan, Wisconsin, Pennsylvania, California, and North Carolina producing the most. (Photograph © Keith Baum)*

duplicate as can be found. We feel exposed, disheveled from channeling the alien tide around our fields. Our muscles ache from securing hundreds of trees with binder twine to hundreds of vehicles.

We survey the decimated fields. The removals seem as scattered and random as the destruction path of a Gulf hurricane. Our faith in the intelligence and goodwill of humankind is confirmed as we note the stumps conscientiously cut as instructed, high enough to preserve the lowest branches. Those branches in time will develop buds, the *turnups* that will generate a new tree on the old stump, and will come to maturity much sooner than one grown from seed. Here and there an abandoned specimen, cut and then rejected, reflects a not-so-honorable hand.

The late December tule mist laces the tops of our remaining tree family with shimmering webs as we stow our signs until next year. We retreat into our treasured rural solitude. And experience again that surprised satisfaction at knowing we have a presence in all those living rooms where
"Angers pause in strange regard
For the sweet and gentle madness born
When a wintry sky was starred."

Sleigh Ride in the Country

By Peter McArthur

Poet, humorist, and farmyard philosopher, Peter McArthur was the son of a rural Ontario farmer. He left the farmstead to pursue a college education in Toronto, then spent nearly two decades living in two of the world's largest cities, New York City and London, England, as he followed a career path through journalism, editing, and advertising.

In 1908, at the age of forty-two, McArthur returned to the farm of his youth. Although he had washed his hands of city life, he did not leave behind his wit, imagination, or deft writing ability. He regaled urban dwellers with the details of his life in the countryside—from farm chores to changing seasons—via a regular column in the Toronto *Globe*. Through his essays about piglets, roosters, vegetable gardens, woodpiles, and maple syrup, he kept rich record of rural life in early twentieth-century Canada.

McArthur's writings have been collected into several books, including *In Pastures Green* (1916), from which the following selection was taken. Here McArthur shares the beauty of the snow-covered countryside and the satisfaction found in the traditional Christmas sleigh ride.

Family sleigh outing
An Amish family takes their sleigh for a turn on the snowy Pennsylvania countryside. (Photograph © Keith Baum)

"THE COUNTRY LOOKS just like a Christmas card," said an enthusiast of city breeding, which goes to prove the truth of Whistler's observation that "Nature is looking up." The sleighing came with Christmas and made it perfect. There had been flurries of snow before that had drifted to the hollows and fence-corners, and had given the country a sketchy, unfinished look, but on Christmas morning the fields and roads were covered several inches deep with an even layer of crisp snow. Cutters were dusted and brought out, and before noon there was a constant jingling of bells on the country roads. Ever since there has been good sleighing, and holiday visiting has been worth while, if for no other reason than the drive through the clear, cold air. Even the turkeys and mince-pies and plum-puddings seemed to taste better after an appetising outing with the thermometer at fifteen above. Since the sleighing began the towns have been crowded with visitors from the farms, who were out more for the drive than for any shopping they had to do. As a matter of fact, sleighing is now simply one of the pleasures of the country. There is no more heavy teaming to do, and really practical farmers who look at things from a business point of view would be just as well pleased if we did not have sleighing at all. As long as there is enough snow to protect the wheat they are satisfied. Sleighing makes it necessary to have sleighs and cutters instead of waggons and buggies, and that is an added expense.

Thank heaven, there are still enough inconsequential people living to like sleighing just for the fun of it. They hitch up their roadsters and go out for a spin because they like to feel the exhilaration it gives. May their tribe increase.

As if not satisfied with giving us perfect winter weather, Nature started in yesterday afternoon to show what she can do, when in the mood, to make the world bewilderingly beautiful. Early in the afternoon, wisps of fog began to float across the field and the raw cold proved the truth of the old doggerel:

"A winter fog
Will freeze a dog."

As the fog floated past a fine hoar-frost began to settle everywhere and the sun went down red as in Indian summer. The straggling fog-banks on the horizon began to glow, and we said:

"The low red rim
Of a winter's twilight, crisp and dim."

Then came an hour of darkness and when the full moon rose it lighted a fairyland. Every twig, weed, and exposed blade of grass was frosted to three times its usual thickness with feathery hoar-frost of dazzling whiteness. Only the trunks and larger limbs of the trees remained black. As the stars were blotted out by the light, all except the larger ones and a planet that hung in the west like a drop of liquid silver, the snow began to light up with infinite constellations. There was moonlight and snow "Fur's you cud look or listen." Not a breath of air disturbed the tense stillness. Presently, an owl—

Everybody in?
Left and facing page: *The larger the family, the larger the family sleigh. A carved two-seater and single horse is fine for the family of four. A family of sixteen, however, requires a sleigh with a big box frame, two sets of runners, and extra horsepower in the form of two hearty Clydesdales. (Photograph © J. C. Allen & Son)*

who, no doubt, "for all his feathers, was a-cold" — hooted in the ghostly woods and the sound boomed and echoed weirdly.

"Whoo-hoo-hoo-whoo-oo!"

It seemed the only sound that would be appropriate in that frozen stillness. As the moon rose higher a perfect storm circle that almost broke into rainbow colours formed around it. All night the spectacle lasted, but the wind that came with the dawn scattered the light frost flakes and mingled them with the drifting snow, but all who loved beauty had a chance to see the matchless artistry of

The goblins of the Northland
That teach the gulls to scream
That dance the autumn into dust.
The ages into dream."

It is worth while to take a trip along the side roads where they still have rail fences to see the snowdrifts.

The briars and withered golden-rod stalks form shelters where the drifts can form and be carved into wonderful shapes by the driving wind. Along the main roads where wire fences are in use the drifts do not have a chance, but on the side-lines they can gather and lie undisturbed, save for the tracking of the wild creatures that now more than at any other season "do seek their meat from God." Sprawling rabbit-tracks abound everywhere, and here and there the loosely-woven lacework of quail-tracks may be seen. Where the briars and weeds are thick they bend down under the weight of the drifts, but hold them up sufficiently to provide hiding-places for the rabbits and quail, and shelter them from the cold. Occasionally one sees the jumping track of a weasel or mink that finds in the drifts an ideal hunting-ground. Everywhere flocks of snowbirds swoop down among the weeds to feed, and add their tiny tracks to the strangely-written history of the winter struggle for existence.

Quiet reflection

Overleaf: *A brief trip down a snowy country lane soothes the spirit and invites quiet reflection during a sometimes harried holiday season. (Photograph © Daniel Dempster)*

Chapter 3

Going Home

"The Christmas holidays are really our national Old Home Week. No matter how much the story of Christmas may be told in press and pulpit, and no matter how earnestly its lessons may be taught and listened to, the mastering spell of Christmas is the spell of home. On Christmas Day scattered families are reassembled, cares are put aside and there are feasting and rejoicing that renew the ties of home."
—Peter McArthur, *Around Home*

Since Mary and Joseph returned to his hometown of Bethlehem for the world's first Christmas, it is appropriate that one of the rituals of the Christmas holiday is going home, at least in spirit, if not in body.

"Going home for Christmas" means different things to different people. For some, it means returning to that place where the bulk of their past Christmases have been spent. That place might be the house in which they actually grew up, or it might be a "Christmas home," such as grandparents' farmstead or home of an aunt and uncle—the annual location of the family holiday festivities. Ultimately, "going home" means joining loved ones, wherever they may be gathered.

But a physical return is only one aspect of going home for Christmas. "Going home" also means returning to one's past. It is an annual reunion—sometimes joyful, sometimes anxious—with the people, the lives, and memories that have been left behind.

The selections in this chapter illustrate the varied affects going home can have on those returning to farm country for Christmas.

"Over the river and through the woods . . ."
Left: *No road is more beautiful than the one that takes us home. (Photograph © William Johnson)*

To the Farm and Back

By Paul Engle

To a child going to his grandparents' farm for Christmas, getting there is half the fun—especially because getting there meant going in his father's sleigh. This annual holiday pilgrimage is just one of the childhood reminiscences that fueled the pen of Iowa poet and writer Paul Engle.

The themes and images of Engle's writings are unabashedly American. Known primarily as a poet, he has been praised for his Walt Whitman–esque visions and style. His prosaic works, which include many essays and a single novel, also honor rural life and midwestern America.

Engle's influence on American literature extends well beyond his own contributions, however. In 1942, he became director of the Iowa Writer's Workshop at the University of Iowa, and during the next twenty years he led it to international prominence and fostered the talents of many writers. In 1967, he and his wife Hualing Engle established the International Writing Program at the University of Iowa to encourage conversation between writers throughout the world.

This selection can be found in *An Old Fashioned Christmas* (1964), a collection of Engle's holiday poetry and prose. It celebrates the "going" aspect of "going home."

"They're here!"
The arrival of family and friends signals the beginning of the Christmas Day celebration. (Photograph © J. C. Allen & Son)

EVERY CHRISTMAS SHOULD begin with the sound of bells, and when I was a child mine always did. But they were sleigh bells, not church bells, for we lived in a part of Cedar Rapids, Iowa, where there were no churches. My bells were on my father's team of horses as he drove up to our horse-headed hitching post with the bobsled that would take us to celebrate Christmas on the family farm ten miles out in the country. My father would bring the team down Fifth Avenue at a smart trot, flicking his whip over the horses' rumps and making the bells double their light, thin jangling over the snow, whose radiance threw back a brilliance like the sound of bells.

Whose father now drives up on Christmas morning in such exciting style as mine did when I was a child?

With more anticipation than we would have today waiting for a jet to fly in from Paris, my younger sister and I would stand at a window looking down the street. Kathryn would clap her hands, jump up and down, and cry "There he comes!"

Such speed, such power, it seemed, such a roar of arrival with the runners crunching on the snow, the bells clanging, the horses snorting as father snapped his long whip over their heads! How dull the rubber-skidded arrival of a plane, compared to the rush and clang of steel runners beautifully sliding over ice and snow.

Father would bring the bobsled smartly around in a whirl of snow and prancing feet in the sort of arrival which no plane on a runway and no car on a plowed and paved street could ever imitate. By then my sister and I would have run out to help, holding the reins between us as father tied the team to our hitching post. There was more feeling of motion and flight in our two horsepower, Billy and Buck, than in any hundreds of mechanical horsepower.

Our whole Christmas was that way; there was more life in it, close to animals and to the land, than in our city celebration today. Like most people toward the beginning of this troubled century, we had relatives on the farm.

There are no such departures as ours for that farm any more: the whole family piling into the bobsled with a foot of golden oat straw to lie in and heavy buffalo robes to lie under, the horses stamping the soft snow, and at every motion of their hoofs the bells jingling, jingling. My father sat there with the reins firmly held, wearing a long coat made from the hide of a favorite family horse, the deep chestnut color still glowing, his mittens also from the same hide. It always troubled me as a boy of eight that the horses had so indifferent a view of their late friend appearing as a warm overcoat on the back of the man who put the iron bit in their mouths.

A bobsled was the wonderful and proper way to travel on Christmas morning. The space it offered was generous, like the holiday itself. There was no crowding on narrow seats where children had to sit upright. Instead, the long, wide body allowed us such comfort and freedom as no car or plane can give.

In that abundant dimension, we could burrow down under the clean-smelling straw, pull a shaggy robe over us, and travel warm and snug while still being outdoors with the wind in our faces.

We could hop out and ride on the heavy runners, the snow piling up against our boots and the runners making it seem dangerous as they bounced and twisted over the unpaved streets, making their hissing, tearing sound over the packed snow.

It was a close and intimate Christmas, and like that whole feeling of warm familiarity was the sound of the bobsled's runners. Their expressive noise is gone forever, and no rubber tire hissing on pavement can ever have such exciting variety.

As the runners slid over snow, ice, and an occasional stone or bare spot with dirt, they would carry on a sustained monologue continually changing. They would whisper gently over snow, mutter angrily over ice, squeak over gravel, cry in rage over an exposed rock, then go back to the long rhythm of the glide over hard-packed snow.

That was dramatic travel, just as the horses, alive and individual, each with its own characteristics, were a more exciting source of motive power than a mechanical engine with its stink and noise.

We were close to those horses. My father had bought them young and trained them himself, so that he could drive them with a light hand, as much by the expressive sound of his voice as by a whip on the withers or a bit in the mouth. We would continually urge Billy along as he lagged just enough behind Buck so that he had a little less to pull.

On a level piece of road, Father would collect the reins firmly, cluck to the team, snap the whip over their ears, and settle them into a fast trot, bells

Sun rays and storm clouds
Sun rays shine against storm clouds to produce an eerie cast over this New England farmstead. (Photograph © Stephen R. Swinburne)

jangling in celebration, runners clacking, and the children yelling with the speed and sway of it.

There are no streets like those any more: the snow sensibly left on the road for the sake of sleighs and easy travel. And along the streets we met other horses, so that we moved from one set of bells to another, from the tiny tinkle of the individual bells on the shafts to the silvery, leaping sound of the long strands hung over the harness. There would be an occasional brass-mounted automobile laboring on its narrow tires and as often as not pulled up the slippery hills by a horse, and we would pass it with a triumphant shout for an awkward nuisance which was obviously not here to stay.

The country road ran through a landscape of little hills and shallow valleys and heavy groves of timber, including one of great towering black walnut trees which were all cut down a year later to be made into gunstocks for the First World War. The great moment was when we left the road and turned up the long lane on the farm. It ran through fields where watermelons were always planted in the summer because

of the fine sandy soil, and I could go out and break one open to see its Christmas colors of green skin and red inside. My grandfather had been given some of that farm as bounty land for service as a cavalryman in the Civil War.

My uncle, mother's brother, and our cousins lived on the same place where mother had been born. Somehow, a place of country quiet, with livestock crunching on its feed, with sheds and barns and corncribs, with crop and pasture land rolling away serenely, their shape clearer in winter under the defining snow, seemed the best of all possible places to celebrate this holiday begun in a little village in sheepraising country on the other side of the world.

Near the low house on the hill, with oaks on one side and apple trees on the other, my father would stand up, flourish his whip, and bring the bobsled right up to the door of the house with a burst of speed.

There are no such arrivals any more: the harness bells ringing and clashing, the horses whinnying at the horses in the barn and receiving a great, trumpeting whinny in reply, the dogs leaping into the bobsled

"To Grandmother's house we go . . ."
The warmest part of the farm kitchen is the people who live there. In one simple panel, cartoonist Bob Artley captures the all joy of a family's arrival at grandma and grandpa's farm. During his career as a cartoonist for the Des Moines Register and the Worthington Daily Globe, Artley drew on the memories of his childhood on a farm. (Artwork © Bob Artley)

and burrowing under the buffalo robes, a squawking from the hen house, a yelling of "Whoa, whoa," at the excited horses, boy and girl cousins howling around the bobsled, and the descent into the snow with the Christmas basket carried by my mother.

My Uncle Charlie was certainly not John the Baptist wearing a coat of camel's hair and a leather girdle about his loins. Nor was he preaching "Repent ye: for the kingdom of heaven is at hand."

But standing at the farmhouse door, wearing a heavy sheepskin jacket over his stained overalls, urging us in with a hearty shout of, "Come and set where it's warm," he was certainly a prophet. What he prophesied was good cheer and a gay Christmas. . . .

Penny postcard
The sender of this German-made holiday postcard paid one cent to mail her good wishes in 1910.

After dinner, late in the afternoon, the women would make despairing gestures toward the dirty dishes and scoop up hot water from the reservoir at the side of the range. The men would go to the barn and look after the livestock. My older cousin would take his new .22 rifle and stalk out across the pasture with the remark, "I saw that fox just now looking for his Christmas goose." Or sleds would be dragged out and we would slide in a long snake, feet hooked into the sled behind, down the hill and across the westward sloping fields into the sunset. Bones would be thrown to dogs, suet tied in the oak trees for the juncos and winter-defying chickadees, a saucer of skimmed milk set out for the cats, daintily and disgustedly picking their padded feet through the snow, and crumbs scattered on a bird feeder where already the crimson cardinals would be dropping out of the sky like blood. Then back to the house for a final warming up before leaving.

There was usually a song around the tree before we were all bundled up, many thanks all around for gifts, the basket as loaded as when it came, more so,

for leftover food had been piled in it. My father and uncle would have brought up the team from the barn and hooked them into the double shafts of the bobsled, and we would all go out into the freezing air of early evening. . . .

And now those bells again as the horses, impatient from their long standing in the barn, stamped and shook their harness, my father holding them back with a soft clucking in his throat and a hard pull on the reins. The smell of wood smoke flavoring the air in our noses, the cousins shivering with cold, "Good-by, good-by," called out from everyone, and the bobsled would slide off, creaking over the frost-brittle snow. All of us, my mother included, would dig down in the straw and pull the buffalo robes up to our chins. As the horses settled into a steady trot, the bells gently chiming in their rhythmical beat, we would fall half asleep, the hiss of the runners comforting. As we looked up at the night sky through half-closed eyelids, the constant bounce and swerve of the runners would seem to shake the little stars as if they would fall into our laps. But that one great star in the East never wavered. Nothing could shake it from the sky as we drifted home on Christmas.

Getting there is half the fun

The swish of the runners, the crunch of horses hooves, the jingling of the harness, the rushing of the wind—for pure sensory delight, no other mode of transport beats a sleigh. Of course, before the advent of the automobile and four-wheel drive, sleighs were not only exciting, but also practical, especially in the countryside. Families could easily travel to town, to church, and to other farms in a sleigh—and they didn't need to wait for plows to clear the roads.

(Photography © Bob Firth/Firth Photobank)

A Green Gables Christmas

By L. M. Montgomery

In 1905, while searching for a plot for a magazine serial story, Canadian writer L. M. Montgomery created the character Anne Shirley, a spirited, loquacious young orphan taken in by a quiet farming couple. Her story quickly grew into Montgomery's first and most famous novel, *Anne of Green Gables*. The book's popularity led to six subsequent novels about Anne's life, all full of adventures and characters inspired in part by the author's own personality and life events.

Montgomery had already established a solid writing career, regularly contributing poems, essays, and short stories to newspapers and magazines throughout Canada, before emerging as a novelist. In addition to her tales of Anne, she published nineteen books before her death in 1942; all but one of her books is set on her childhood home of Prince Edward Island.

The following excerpt comes from *Anne of Windy Poplars* (1936). Anne is now a young college woman returning to the farm of Green Gables for a holiday reunion with her adoptive mother Marilla, Marilla's live-in friend Rachel Lynde, Anne's adoptive "brother and sister" Davy and Dora, and her beloved fiancé Gilbert. She has asked Katherine, a rather prickly acquaintance, to join her, anticipating—correctly—that the beauty and warm spirit of Christmas at Green Gables will work magic on Katherine's chilly heart.

Welcome home
A farmstead patiently waits at the end of the lane for family and friends to return. (Photography © Keith Baum)

ANNE WAS ALREADY tasting Christmas happiness. She fairly sparkled as the train left the station. The ugly streets slipped past her . . . she was going home . . . home to Green Gables. Out in the open country the world was all golden-white and pale violet, woven here and there with the dark magic of spruces and the leafless delicacy of birches. The low sun behind the bare woods seemed rushing through the trees like a splendid god, as the train sped on. Katherine was silent but did not seem ungracious.

"Don't expect me to talk," she had warned Anne curtly.

"I won't. I hope you don't think I'm one of those terrible people who make you feel that you *have* to talk to them all the time. We'll just talk when we feel like it. I admit I'm likely to feel like it a good part of the time, but you're under no obligation to take any notice of what I'm saying."

Davy met them at Bright River with a big two-seated sleigh full of furry robes . . . and a bear hug for Anne. The two girls snuggled down in the back seat. The drive from the station to Green Gables had always been a very pleasant part of Anne's weekends home. She always recalled her first drive home from Bright River with Matthew. That had been in spring and this was December, but everything along the road kept saying to her, "Do you remember?" The snow crisped under the runners; the music of the bells tinkled through the ranks of tall pointed firs, snow-laden. The White Way of Delight had little festoons of stars tangled in the trees. And on the last hill but one they saw the great gulf, white and mystical under the moon but not yet ice-bound.

"There's just one spot on this road where I always feel suddenly . . . 'I'm *home*,'" said Anne. "It's the top of the next hill, where we'll see the lights of Green Gables. I'm just thinking of the supper Marilla will have ready for us. I believe I can smell it here. Oh, it's good . . . good . . . good to be home again!"

At Green Gables every tree in the yard seemed to welcome her back . . . every lighted window was beckoning. And how good Marilla's kitchen smelled as they opened the door. There were hugs and exclamations and laughter. Even Katherine seemed somehow no outsider, but one of them. Mrs. Rachel Lynde had set her cherished parlor lamp on the supper-table and lighted it. It was really a hideous thing with a hideous red globe, but what a warm rosy becoming light it cast over everything! How warm and friendly were the shadows! How pretty Dora was growing! And Davy really seemed almost a man.

There was news to tell. Diana had a small daughter . . . Josie Pye actually had a young man . . . and Charlie Sloane was said to be engaged. It was all just as exciting as news of empire could have been. Mrs. Lynde's new patchwork quilt, just completed, containing five thousand pieces, was on display and received its meed of praise.

"When you come home, Anne," said Davy, "everything seems to come alive."

"Ah, this is how life should be," purred Dora's kitten.

"I've always found it hard to resist the lure of a moonlight night," said Anne after supper. "How about a snowshoe tramp, Miss Brooke? I think that I've heard that you snowshoe."

"Yes . . . it's the only thing I *can* do . . . but I haven't done it for six years," said Katherine with a shrug.

Anne rooted out her snow-shoes from the garret and Davy shot over to Orchard Slope to borrow an old pair of Diana's for Katherine. They went through Lover's Lane, full of lovely tree shadows, and across fields where little fir trees fringed the fences and through woods which were full of secrets they seemed always on the point of whispering to you but never did . . . and through open glades that were like pools of silver.

They did not talk or want to talk. It was as if they were afraid to talk for fear of spoiling something beautiful. But Anne had never felt so *near* Katherine Brooke before. By some magic of its own the winter night had brought them together . . . *almost* together but not quite.

When they came out to the main road and a sleigh flashed by, bells ringing, laughter tinkling, both girls gave an involuntary sigh. It seemed to both that they were leaving behind a world that had nothing in common with the one to which they were returning . . . a world where time was not . . . which was young with immortal youth . . . where souls communed with each

Nuthatch ornaments
Outdoor Christmas tree ornaments attract the attention of a white-breasted nuthatch. (Photograph © Leonard Lee Rue III)

other in some medium that needed nothing so crude as words.

"It's been wonderful," said Katherine so obviously to herself that Anne made no response.

They went down the road and up the long Green Gables lane but just before they reached the yard gate, they both paused as by a common impulse and stood in silence, leaning against the old mossy fence and looked at the brooding motherly old house seen dimly through its veil of trees. How beautiful Green Gables was on a winter night! . . .

Saturday and Monday were full of gay doings at Green Gables. The plum pudding was concocted and the Christmas tree brought home. Katherine and Anne and Davy and Dora went to the woods for it . . . a beautiful little fir to whose cutting down Anne was only reconciled by the fact that it was in a little clearing of Mr. Harrison's which was going to be stumped and plowed in the spring anyhow.

They wandered about, gathering creeping spruce and ground pine for wreaths . . . even some ferns that kept green in a certain deep hollow of the woods all winter . . . until day smiled back at night over white-bosomed hills and they came back to Green Gables in triumph . . . to meet a tall young man with hazel eyes and the beginnings of a mustache which made him look so much older and maturer that Anne had one awful moment of wondering if it were really Gilbert or a stranger.

Katherine, with a little smile that tried to be sarcastic but couldn't quite succeed, left them in the parlor and played games with the twins in the kitchen all the evening. To her amazement she found she was enjoying it. And what fun it was to go down cellar with Davy and find that there were really such things as sweet apples still left in the world.

Katherine had never been in a country cellar before and had no idea what a delightful, spooky, shadowy place it could be by candle-light. Life already seemed *warmer*. For the first time it came home to Katherine that life might be beautiful, even for her.

Davy made enough noise to wake the Seven Sleepers, at an unearthly hour Christmas morning, ringing

Pastel sunset
A bright clear day gives way to a pastel sunset over frosted willows and frozen fields. (Photograph © Scott T. Smith)

©Sandi Wickersham Resnick.

an old cowbell up and down the stairs. Marilla was horrified at his doing such a thing when there was a guest in the house, but Katherine came down laughing. Somehow, an odd camaraderie had sprung up between her and Davy. She told Anne candidly that she had no use for the impeccable Dora but that Davy was somehow tarred with her own brush.

They opened the parlor and distributed the gifts before breakfast because the twins, even Dora, couldn't have eaten anything if they hadn't. Katherine, who had not expected anything except, perhaps, a duty gift from Anne, found herself getting presents from every one. A gay, crocheted afghan from Mrs. Lynde . . . a sachet of orris root from Dora . . . a paperknife from Davy . . . a basketful of tiny jars of jam and jelly from Marilla . . . even a little bronze cheesy cat for a paper-weight from Gilbert.

And, tied under the tree, curled up on a bit of warm and woolly blanket, a dear little brown-eyed puppy, with alert, silken ears and an ingratiating tail. A card tied to his neck bore the legend, "From Anne, who dares, after all, to wish you a Merry Christmas."

Katherine gathered his wriggling little body up in her arms and spoke shakily.

"Anne . . . he's a darling! But Mrs. Dennis won't let me keep him. I asked her if I might get a dog and she refused."

"I've arranged it all with Mrs. Dennis. You'll find she won't object. And, anyway, Katherine, you're not going to be there long. You *must* find a decent place to live, now that you've paid off what you thought were your obligations. Look at the lovely box of stationery Diana sent me. Isn't it fascinating to look at the blank pages and wonder what will be written on them?"

Mrs. Lynde was thankful it was a white Christmas . . . there would be no fat graveyards when Christmas was white . . . but to Katherine it seemed a purple and crimson and golden Christmas. And the week that followed was just as beautiful. Katherine had often wondered bitterly just what it would be like to be happy

Not the same old grind
Virginia artist Sandi Wickersham's memories of her childhood growing up on a farm come to life in her paintings. Having grown up in a family of storytellers, she now tells her own stories using vivid color and a keen eye for detail. (Artwork © Sandi Wickersham)

Frozen Farmall
A 1930s International Harvester Farmall F-12 waits out the winter. (Photograph © Paul Rezendes)

and now she found out. She bloomed out in the most astonishing way. Anne found herself enjoying their companionship.

"To think I was afraid she would spoil my Christmas holiday!" she reflected in amazement.

"To think," said Katherine to herself, "that I was on the verge of refusing to come here when Anne invited me!"

They went for long walks . . . through Lover's Lane and the Haunted Wood, where the very silence seemed friendly . . . over hills where the light snow whirled in a winter dance of goblins . . . through old orchards full of violet shadows . . . through the glory of sunset woods. There were no birds to chirp or sing, no brooks to gurgle, no squirrels to gossip. But the wind made occasional music that had in quality what it lacked in quantity.

"One can always find something lovely to look at or listen to," said Anne.

They talked of "cabbages and kings," and hitched their wagons to stars, and came home with appetites that taxed even the Green Gables pantry. One day it stormed and they couldn't go out. The east wind was beating around the eaves and the gray gulf was roaring. But even a storm at Green Gables had charms of its own. It was cozy to sit by the stove and dreamily watch the firelight flickering over the ceiling while you munched apples and candy. How jolly supper was with the storm wailing outside! . . .

There was a concert in the hall one night, with a party at Abner Sloane's after it, and Anne persuaded Katherine to go to both.

"I want you to give us a reading for our program, Katherine. I've heard you read beautifully."

"I used to recite . . . I think I rather liked doing it. But the summer before last I recited at a shore concert which a party of summer resorters got up . . . and I heard them laughing at me afterwards."

"How do you know they were laughing at you?"

"They must have been. There wasn't anything else to laugh at."

Anne hid a smile and persisted in asking for the reading. . . .

Katherine finally promised the reading but was dubious about the party. "I'll go, of course. But nobody will ask me to dance and I'll feel sarcastic and preju-diced and ashamed. I'm always miserable at parties . . . the few I've ever gone to. Nobody seems to think I can dance . . . and you know I can fairly well, Anne. I picked it up at Uncle Henry's, because a poor bit of a maid they had wanted to learn, too, and she and I used to dance together in the kitchen at night to the music that went on in the parlor. I think I'd like it . . . with the right kind of partner."

"You won't be miserable at this party, Katherine. You won't be outside looking in. There's all the difference in the world, you know, between being inside looking out and outside looking in. You have such lovely hair, Katherine. Do you mind if I try a new way of doing it?"

Katherine shrugged.

"Oh, go ahead. I suppose my hair does look dreadful . . . but I've no time to be always primping. I haven't a party dress. Will my green taffeta do?"

"It will have to do . . . though green is the one color above all others that you should never wear, my Katherine. But you're going to wear a red, pin-tucked chiffon collar I've made for you. Yes, you *are*. You ought to have a red dress, Katherine."

"I've always hated red. When I went to live with Uncle Henry, Aunt Gertrude always made me wear aprons of bright Turkey-red. The other children in school used to call out 'Fire,' when I came in with one of those aprons on. Anyway, I can't be bothered with clothes."

"Heaven grant me patience! Clothes are *very* important," said Anne severely, as she braided and coiled. Then she looked at her work and saw that it was good. She put her arm about Katherine's shoulders and turned her to the mirror.

"Don't you truly think we are a pair of quite good-looking girls?" she laughed. "And isn't it really nice to think people will find some pleasure in looking at us? There are so many homely people who would actually look quite attractive if they took a little pains with themselves. Three Sundays ago in church . . . you remember the day poor old Mr. Milvain preached and had such a terrible cold in his head that nobody could make out what he was saying? . . . well, I passed the time making the people around me beautiful. I gave Mrs. Brent a new nose, I waved Mary Addison's hair and gave Jane Marden's a lemon rinse . . . I dressed Emma Dill in blue instead of brown . . . I dressed Charlotte Blair in stripes instead of checks . . . I removed several moles . . . and I shaved off Thomas Anderson's long, sandy Piccadilly weepers. You couldn't have known them when I got through with them. And, except perhaps for Mrs. Brent's nose, they could have done everything I did, themselves. Why, Katherine, your eyes are just the color of tea . . . amber tea. Now, live up to your name this evening . . . a brook should be sparkling . . . limpid . . . merry."

"Everything I'm not."

"Everything you've been this past week. So you *can* be it."

"That's only the magic of Green Gables. When I go back to Summerside, twelve o'clock will have struck for Cinderella."

"You'll take the magic back with you. Look at yourself . . . looking for once as you ought to look all the time."

Katherine gazed at her reflection in the mirror as if rather doubting her identity.

"I do look years younger," she admitted. "You were right . . . clothes *do* do things to you. Oh, I know I've been looking older than my age. I didn't care. Why should I? Nobody else cared. And I'm not like you, Anne. Apparently you were born knowing how to live. And I don't know anything about it . . . not even the A B C. I wonder if it's too late to learn. I've been sarcastic so long, I don't know if I can be anything else. Sarcasm seemed to me to be the only way I could make any impression on people. And it seems to me, too, that I've always been afraid when I was in the company of other people . . . afraid of saying something stupid . . . afraid of being laughed at."

"Katherine Brooke, look at yourself in that mirror; carry that picture of yourself with you . . . magnificent hair framing your face instead of trying to pull it backward . . . eyes sparkling like dark stars . . . a little flush of excitement on your cheeks . . . and you won't feel afraid. Come, now. We're going to be late, but fortunately all the performers have what I heard Dora referring to as 'preserved' seats."

Gilbert drove them to the hall. How like old times it was . . . only Katherine was with her in place of Diana. Anne sighed. Diana had so many other interests now. No more running round to concerts and parties for her.

But what an evening it was! What silvery satin roads with a pale green sky in the west after a light snowfall! Orion was treading his stately march across the heavens, and hills and fields and woods lay around them in a pearly silence.

Katherine's reading captured her audience from the first line, and at the party she could not find dances for all her would-be partners. She suddenly found herself laughing without bitterness. Then home to Green Gables, warming their toes at the sitting-room fire by the light of two friendly candles on the mantel; and Mrs. Lynde tiptoeing into their room, late as it was, to ask them if they'd like another blanket and assure Katherine that her little dog was snug and warm in a basket behind the kitchen stove.

"I've got a new outlook on life," thought Katherine as she drifted off to slumber. "I didn't know there were people like this."

Is there one for me?
A young Jack Russell terrier, sporting the latest in holiday puppy wear, wonders if Santa Claus brought him the squeaky chew toy he requested. (Photograph © J. C. Allen & Son)

Christmas Exiles

By Garrison Keillor

Writer, radio personality, humorist—Garrison Keillor's work has earned him all these titles.

His essays and columns frequently appear in magazines such as the *New Yorker, Atlantic Monthly,* and *Time*. But it is his public radio program *A Prairie Home Companion* that has made Keillor's words a mainstay in households throughout the country. Since the show's debut in 1974 on Minnesota Public Radio, he has written each of the show's monologues and sketches himself and taken millions of listeners to visit Lake Wobegon, Minnesota, a country town "that time forgot and decades cannot improve."

Lake Wobegon is also the setting for three of Keillor's ten books. The words, lifestyles, and beliefs of the town's residents resonate with those who have spent any part of their lives in small, rural, Midwestern areas—and that ring of truth is what makes his stories humorous.

Anyone who has returned home to find a farm country Christmas that is somewhat less than festive will recognize the exiles in the following excerpts from Keillor's 1987 book *Leaving Home*.

There's no place like home
An old saying contends that "you can't go home again," but every year the Christmas holiday compels many people to try. (Photograph © J. C. Allen & Son)

It has been a quiet week in Lake Wobegon. Christmas. The exiles were home. It was pretty quiet, though you could hear the gritting of teeth, and there was a moment of poisoned silence at the Clarence Bunsen home that rang like a fire bell. Before the blessing, as they sat around the table and admired the work in front of them, a still-life *Christmas Dinner* by Arlene, before they ate the art, their daughter, Donna, in town from San Diego, said, "What a wonderful Christmas!" and her husband, Rick, said, "Well, if Democrats had their way, it'd be the last one." Silence.

Arlene said that if Rick had his way, the turkeys would be having us. Clarence bowed his head. "Dear Lord, the giver of all good things, we thank Thee." He prayed a long prayer, as a cease-fire. Arlene smiled at Rick: "Have some mashed potatoes." "Thank you, Mom." She winced. He is her son-in-law and she doesn't know why. He is not raising her grandchildren right, he comes to Minnesota and talks too much about the advantages of southern California, he wears silly clothes, he makes fun of Norwegians, he makes fun of women including his own wife, and he says "agenda" in place of "plan" — "Did you have a different agenda?" he says. "Let's get our agenda straight." "I sense a hidden agenda here."

He piled his plate with Christmas agenda and chomped a big bite of it. He said, "Mom, this is the best dinner I ever ate. I really mean that." She smiled her brightest smile, the smile she has used all her life on people she'd like to slap silly. She'd like to give him a piece of her mind, but she can't because he has hostages, her grandchildren. So she kills him with kindness. She stuffs him like a turkey. Fresh caramel rolls for breakfast, a pound of bacon and smoked sausage and scrambled eggs, and two hours later pot roast for lunch and big slabs of banana cream pie. He has gained four pounds since Tuesday. Her goal is twelve. All day he sits dazed by food. "Fudge bars, Rick? I made them just for you. Here, I'll put the plate right beside you, where you can reach them." "Oh Mom . . . " She's found the crack in his armor, and it's his mouth. His Achilles mouth. Her agenda is stuffing him so he becomes weak and pliable and goes into a calorie coma, and she takes the boy and the girl for walks and tells them about our great presidents, our great Democratic presidents. And did you know they were all Norwegian? Yes, they were, a little bit, on their mother's side, and that little bit was enough to make them great.

* * * *

At the Tolleruds', Daryl and Marilyn and their six kids went up the hill to the folks' house. His brothers, Gunnar and Fred, and their families were home for Christmas, and Daryl's family barely has room for themselves around their little table.

When Daryl went into farming in partnership with his dad in 1968, he was under the impression that someday soon he and Marilyn would move into the big house and the folks would take the little one, the one that Grandpa Tollerud built when he came from Norway. But nothing has been said about this for a long time. The little house would be fine for an older couple, who tend to sit quietly and not tear around chasing each other. But the old folks sit quietly in the big house, with four empty bedrooms upstairs. "We really need a larger house," Daryl says. "Well," his dad says. "Soon as we get the pig barn built we'll see about adding on to it."

Up at the folks' house, Christmas is the exact same as it's been forever. You close your eyes and it could be any time. You might open them and you'd be six years old, not forty-two. The dialogue is the same. His mother complains about leaving the turkey in the oven too long and it being too dry, and every year it is perfect. The men sit in the living room, gently clearing their throats, and when it's time, his dad stands up and says, "Well, I'm going to go see to the horse."

They haven't kept a horse for years. "You boys going to come help me see to the horse?" he says, and they troop out to the barn and he reaches down behind a horse collar and pulls out the bottle of Jim Beam. They pass it around and have a pull, and stand and say some things, and pass it around again, and the old man takes a nail and marks the new level and puts it back, and they troop indoors. Daryl wishes they could just have a drink in the living room, but to his old man there's a difference. He is not the sort of man who keeps booze in his house. The barn doesn't count. . . .

Daryl was depressed for two days. Tuesday night he left a door open in the pig barn, and twelve got out. Recess for pigs. It took him and Eric two hours to get them back in class, but Daryl felt fast on his feet and felt the reflexes working, bang, bang, bang. Wednesday afternoon, not thinking, he walked in the kitchen and opened the fridge and got out a bowl that was full of glop and dumped it in the garbage, and just as the

The sentinal

A Holstein keeps a look out for visitors to Vermont's Liberty Hill Farm. (Photograph © Lynn Stone)

force of gravity was pulling it down he thought, "That's mincemeat pie filling."

How could he do such a dumb thing? Just wasn't thinking. Marilyn was gone to the farm wives' luncheon. It was two o'clock. He had never made mincemeat filling before, but how hard could it be to follow a recipe? Fairly hard, he discovered. Mincing the meat. Beef and venison. Mincing the apples. And then the recipe called for brandy. No brandy anywhere that he could find—where did she keep the stuff? Did she have a secret stash in the laundry room? Finally he took an empty mustard jar in his pocket and snuck up the hill to the barn. He crawled around back through the corn, dashed for the door, got the bottle, filled the

jar, made a careful mark with the nail. Heard a door slam. Tore out back. Crawled through the corn to the end of the field, stood up, walked down to the house, whistling. Into the kitchen. Tossed in the whiskey. Mixed it, cooked it up, popped it in the fridge as the car rolled up the driveway.

Thursday, as they came to dessert, Daryl's heart was pounding. He chose pumpkin. Everyone else chose mincemeat, except Gunnar, who chose pumpkin too. The pie was sliced and served and the first forkfuls of mincemeat came to their mouths. "Mmmmmmm," said his mother. "Oh Marilyn." His dad said, "Oh my, now that's mincemeat." "It sure is," said Fred. "How do you make it, Marilyn?" "Oh, it's

just from a recipe," she said. "Do you use brandy in it?" "Oh no," she said. "You don't really need brandy. I just leave the brandy out." "Well, it's the best I ever ate," said Fred's wife. "You ought to have some of this, Daryl." "No," Daryl said. "I got my pumpkin here. I don't care for mincemeat. Keeps me awake at night. I can't take so much rich food anymore. I'm getting old, I guess."

Corinne Ingqvist came home for Christmas on Sunday. She came barreling north in her red VW from Minneapolis, arguing with a preacher on the radio, telling him his theology was repressive, when she noticed she was going seventy-five mph. She cruised through the lights of town and turned down the long-familiar driveway to their house by the lake. In the backseat were two tins of tea for gifts and 132 critical essays by her seventeen-year-old students on Robert Frost's poem "The Road Not Taken" ("Two roads diverged in a yellow wood, . . . and I—I took the one less traveled by, And that has made all the difference") that she was planning to grade on Monday. Her parents' house seemed like a quiet retreat with only her and Hjalmar and Virginia for Christmas.

She pulled up the driveway and parked by the old limestone wall. She got out the shopping bag of presents and essays and walked up three steps to the back door and put her bare hand on the cold brass knob and a sudden cold thought came to mind: *This soon shall pass. And it won't be too long.* She swayed slightly and then went in. "Hello," said Hjalmar, and kissed her. "Hello, dear, you look so wonderful," said Virginia. The tree in the same place, beside the old piano, in front of the bright fish tank. Orange and silver guppies seemed to swim among the ornaments, drifting to and fro, like orange and silver snowflakes that never reach the ground, fish in the branches among the lights.

Dozens of exiles returned for Christmas. At Our Lady of Perpetual Responsibility, Father Emil roused himself from bed, where he's been down with cancer since Columbus Day, and said Christmas Eve Mass. He was inspired by the sight of all the lapsed Catholics parading into church with their unbaptized children, and he gave them a hard homily, strolling right down into the congregation. "Shame. Shame on us for leaving what we were given that was true and good," he said. "To receive a great treasure in our younger days and to abandon it so that we can lie down in the mud with swine." He stood, one hand on the back of a pew, and everyone in that pew—children of this church who grew up and moved away and did well and now tell humorous stories at parties about Father Emil and what it was like to grow up Catholic—all of them shuddered a little, afraid he might grab them by their Harris-tweed collars and stand them up and ask them questions. "What a sham. What a shame." They came for Christmas, to hear music and see the candles and smell incense and feel hopeful, and here was their old priest with hair in his ears whacking them around—was it a brain cancer he had? *Shame, shame on us.* He looked around at all the little children he'd given first communion to, now grown heavy and prosperous and sad and indolent, but clever enough to explain their indolence and sadness as a rebellion against orthodoxy, a protest, adventurous, intellectual, which really was only dullness of spirit. He stopped. It was so quiet you could hear them not breathing. Then he said that this was why Our Lord had come, to rescue us from dullness of spirit, and so the shepherds had found and so shall we, and then it was Christmas again.

Dozens of exiles were back, including some whom their families weren't expecting because they'd said they weren't coming, couldn't come, were sorry but it was just out of the question. But Christmas exerts powerful forces. We turn a corner in a wretched shopping mall and some few bars of a tune turn a switch in our heads and gates open and tons of water thunder through Hoover Dam, the big turbines spin, electricity flows, and we get in our car and go back, like salmon. . . .

Corinne put off grading those papers until Monday and got busy baking cookies and some little currant buns from an old Norwegian recipe. She hadn't had them since she was little, and now she was baking them herself. Amazing: a delicious smell from childhood that brings back every sweet old aunt and grandma as if they're there beside you, and you do it

Church wreaths

Holiday wreaths adorn the doors of an Episcopal church in Maine. (Photograph © Paul Rezendes)

Opening presents

Although most families who celebrate Christmas maintain the tradition of giving gifts, when and how those gifts are opened varies from household to household. Some families open presents on Christmas Eve, while others wait until first thing Christmas morning or after the holiday dinner. Some distribute and open packages one at a time; in other families, everyone opens their packages all at once in a cacophony of tearing paper and exclamations. (Photograph © J. C. Allen & Son)

with just a little saffron. Monday night she made herself start those papers, and then carolers came, and it wasn't until Tuesday afternoon that she really faced up to it, 132 essays of five hundred words each, about seventy thousand words about the poem "Two roads diverged in a yellow wood, . . . and I—I took the one less traveled by, And that has made all the difference." And of those words at least ten thousand were *I, me, or mine—This poem makes me think of what happened to me when I was ten and my parents said to me . . .* For them, all roads converged into the first person singular. It was hard reading, very hard, and their teacher finally chose the road that led away from the stack of essays toward the Christmas tree and the fish tank. A lovely thing about Christmas is that it's compulsory, like a thunderstorm, and we all go through it together, it's not individual, it's sociable.

Foxy the Proud Boy came home, but now he is Richard to everyone, except among his close pals in the grain-futures business in Minneapolis, where he is Pinky. He drove up in a pink 1987 Ferlinghetti, a car so fabulous that when he sits in it, even en route to his origins in a little house painted lavatory green, he feels attractive and *special*. He forgets his dull seedy relatives, who come out and look at his fantastic car, its red leather seats, the incredible instrument panel that shows you the tides, the movements of planets and galaxies. They peer in the tinted windows and say, "Cheess, there's no room in there, Richard—two seats—what are you thinking of—whaddaya do when you got things to haul?" They don't see that Richard is traveling light, he's secure in himself, and with Vanessa sitting next to him, that's a total reality and his life is complete, and yet—Why does he turn pale

Red on red
What decorations could be more appropriate for a big red International Harvester 1586 than strings of red lights? (Photograph © Paul Rezendes)

when he leads this fabulous woman in a silver-lamé shirt into the dim little house? Why does he tremble? Is it the pictures on the walls: the praying hands, the *Threshers* by Millet, a Winslow Homer ship, needlepoint, "Ve Get Too Soon Oldt and Too Late Schmardt"? Is it his family, who never learned the art of making conversation because they only talk to people they know? A slow and terrible death, asphyxiation in your own past. All afternoon he's dying to get back in the Ferlinghetti and go home. At the first decent opportunity, he begins the long ritual goodbye: Well, I guess it's time we . . . No, really, Ma. Vanessa has to (lie lie lie). Well, okay, just one, but then we got to (lie). No, I'd like to but we promised these friends we'd (lie lie). Finally, with a wave and a roar, they pull away and she turns to Richard the Proud and says, "They were nice. I liked them." But his eyes are

full of tears, from exhaustion and relief and guilt and from pride—he really does love this car, it gives him so much pleasure.

Corinne didn't see Richard, Larry, or Eddie. She stayed home. On Christmas Eve, she and Hjalmar and Virginia sat and talked and listened to the Mormon Tabernacle Choir, both sides, A and B, and their old scratchy record of Lionel Barrymore in *A Christmas Carol*. They watched Midnight Mass from Saint Patrick's Cathedral in New York and ate the saffron buns. In the morning, Hjalmar took their dog, Puddles, for a walk. A mile away, the old dog was exhausted. Hjalmar had to pick him up and carry him home. Hjalmar was too tired to drive into Saint Cloud to the Powers Hotel for the elegant Christmas buffet, and so, because there were only three of them, Corinne said, "Let's not fuss, let's make a little turkey dinner with the microwave Daddy got you for Christmas last year." "Fine," Virginia said, "it's under the bed in the guest room, in the box." They both studied the operating manual. In its attempt to describe the incredible flexibility of the microwave, its various functions and options and alternatives, the infinite variety and joy of the thing, it bewildered them. The control panel had buttons numbered from 0 to 9 and other buttons that said: Over, Stop, Clear, From, Time, Recall, Auto, Memory. Which brought back the memory of how lovely it was to put water in a pot, boil it, and drop stuff in—"No!" Corinne cried. "We can't let electronics defeat us!" They put the frozen turkey-dinner pouches in the microwave, pushed a combination of buttons that made the light go on and the fan whirr, and left the kitchen and went and conversed until the bell rang, but something was wrong: the peas were a bluish green, the pouch of turkey had flecks of silvery ash in it. They had each had two glasses of sherry and were in a philosophical mood. Corinne looked at her mother, her mother looked at Corinne. "Well," said Corinne, "I'll never have babies." "So," said Virginia, "I'll never be a grandma." "That's life," they said, "let's go to David and Judy's and see what Christian charity really is worth nowadays. They invited us, didn't they—? It was a month ago and we said no, but we didn't know then what we know now, so let's go."

The Reverend David Ingqvist and wife, Judith, were in the midst of an argument when they heard the knock on the door. They were arguing whether she is always wrong or not: she was saying that, yes, she can never do anything right, and never pleases him, and he was saying that, no, she was wrong now but she is usually right and, no, she often pleases him and, yes, he does tell her—when he opened the door, expecting to find someone with a gift in hand, and saw his aunt and uncle and cousin. "Hello," said Hjalmar. "We thought we'd come down." "How are you?" said Virginia. "Merry Christmas." "What're you having for dinner?" asked Corinne. "Aren't you going to invite us in?"

Candlelight service
A Christmas Eve candlelight service is a tradition in many churches. The candle flames symbolize the light the Christ child brought to the world and their warmth represents love. (Photograph © William Johnson)

Chapter 4

Classic Celebrations

*"In the age of pseudo-holidays, Christmas was always a real
holiday at the Kohn farm. The day itself was a pandemonious
stirring of memories, and it had the kind of rituals that forced you
to recall and compare each new Christmas to all those of the past."*
—Howard Kohn, *The Last Farmer: An American Memoir*

No matter where they take place, the best farm country
Christmas celebrations include a few quintessential details: a massive Christmas Day dinner, a clamorous tangle of
relatives, and children eagerly awaiting gift-opening time. The
selections in this chapter all pay tribute to the classic farm
country Christmas and its hallmarks.

A classic carol such as "Joy to the World" sung by young
children in a country school Christmas program sounds very
different than "Joy to the World" sung by the Mormon Tabernacle Choir. In the same way, each writer renders his or her
story of Christmas celebrations with a unique voice.

Christmas Day dinner
*The highlight of nearly every farm country Christmas is Christmas
Day dinner, with the whole family gathered around the table for the
feast. (Photograph © J. C. Allen & Son)*

A Farmer Boy's Christmas

By Laura Ingalls Wilder

Laura Ingalls Wilder is known around the world as the author and central character of the beloved series of "Little House" books. Her novels tell a timeless story of a girl's journey into womanhood, but they also serve as a journal of pioneer life and families in nineteenth-century America.

Because she wrote her books for readers who were eight to twelve years old, Wilder's writing style is modest and uncomplicated. The beauty of her stories comes from the richness of details—vivid, honest pictures of the hardships early American settlers overcame as they moved westward, combined with clear yet intricate descriptions of their everyday lives and work.

Although most of her books follow the course of her own life, Wilder's second novel, *Farmer Boy* (1933), recounts her husband Almanzo's childhood on a farm in upstate New York. The following chapter from the book describes Christmas on the Wilder family farm and farmer boy Almanzo's view of the preparations and activities.

Pitching in
A great deal of work goes into preparing for the holiday, and everyone on the farm pitches in to help.
(Photograph © J. C. Allen & Son)

FOR A LONG time it seemed that Christmas would never come. On Christmas, Uncle Andrew and Aunt Delia, Uncle Wesley and Aunt Lindy, and all the cousins were coming to dinner. It would be the best dinner of the whole year. And a good boy might get something in his stocking. Bad boys found nothing but switches in their stockings on Christmas morning. Almanzo tried to be good for so long that he could hardly stand the strain.

But at last it was the day before Christmas and Alice and Royal and Eliza Jane were home again. The girls were cleaning the whole house, and Mother was baking. Royal helped Father with the threshing, but Almanzo had to help in the house. He remembered the switch, and tried to be willing and cheerful.

He had to scour the steel knives and forks, and polish the silver. He had to wear an apron around his neck. He took the scouring-brick and scraped a pile of red dust off it, and then with a wet cloth he rubbed the dust up and down on the knives and forks.

The kitchen was full of delicious smells. Newly baked bread was cooling, frosted cakes and cookies and mince pies and pumpkin pies filled the pantry shelves, cranberries bubbled on the stove. Mother was making dressing for the goose.

Outdoors, the sun was shining on the snow. The icicles twinkled all along the eaves. Far away sleigh-bells faintly jingled, and from the barns came the joyful thud-thud! thud-thud! of the flails. But when all the steel knives and forks were done, Almanzo soberly polished the silver.

Then he had to run to the attic for sage; he had to run down cellar for apples, and upstairs again for onions. He filled the woodbox. He hurried in the cold to fetch water from the pump. He thought maybe he was through, then, anyway for a minute. But no; he had to polish the dining-room side of the stove.

"Do the parlor side yourself, Eliza Jane," Mother said. "Almanzo might spill the blacking."

Almanzo's insides quaked. He knew what would happen if Mother knew about that black splotch, hidden on the parlor wall. He didn't want to get a switch in his Christmas stocking, but he would far rather find a switch there than have Father take him to the woodshed.

That night everyone was tired, and the house was so clean and neat that nobody dared touch anything. After supper Mother put the stuffed, fat goose and the little pig into the heater's oven to roast slowly all night. Father set the dampers and wound the clock. Almanzo and Royal hung clean socks on the back of a chair, and Alice and Eliza Jane hung stockings on the back of another chair.

Then they all took candles and went to bed.

It was still dark when Almanzo woke up. He felt excited, and then he remembered that this was Christmas morning. He jerked back the covers and jumped onto something alive that squirmed. It was Royal. He had forgotten that Royal was there, but he scrambled over him, yelling:

"Christmas! Christmas! Merry Christmas!"

He pulled his trousers over his nightshirt. Royal jumped out of bed and lighted the candle. Almanzo grabbed the candle, and Royal shouted:

"Hi! Leave that be! Where's my pants?"

But Almanzo was already running downstairs. Alice and Eliza Jane were flying from their room, but Almanzo beat them. He saw his sock hanging all lumpy; he set down the candle and grabbed his sock. The first thing he pulled out was a cap, a boughten cap!

The plaid cloth was machine-woven. So was the lining. Even the sewing was machine-sewing. And the ear-muffs were buttoned over the top.

Almanzo yelled. He had not even hoped for such a cap. He looked at it, inside and out; he felt the cloth and the sleek lining. He put the cap on his head. It was a little large, because he was growing. So he could wear it a long time.

Eliza Jane and Alice were digging into their stockings and squealing, and Royal had a silk muffler. Almanzo thrust his hand into his sock again, and pulled out a nickel's worth of horehound candy. He bit off the end of one stick. The outside melted like maple sugar, but the inside was hard and could be sucked for hours.

Then he pulled out a new pair of mittens. Mother had knit the wrists and backs in a fancy stitch. He pulled out an orange, and he pulled out a little package of dried figs. And he thought that was all. He thought no boy ever had a better Christmas.

But in the toe of the sock there was still something more. It was small and thin and hard. Almanzo couldn't imagine what it was. He pulled it out, and it was a jack-knife. It had four blades.

Almanzo yelled and yelled. He snapped all the

Family time
Spending time with the family is one of the best aspects of the Christmas season. (Photograph © J. C. Allen & Son)

A joyful and festive occasion
"One custom that I feel sure will survive for as long as family farming remains a part of the American scene is the country Christmas. It is a joyful and festive occasion. . . ." —Leonard Hall, Country Year: A Journal of the Seasons at Possum Trot Farm. *(Photograph © Paul Rezendes)*

blades open, sharp and shining, and he yelled,

"Alice, look! Look, Royal! Lookee, lookee my jack-knife! Lookee my cap!"

Father's voice came out of the dark bedroom and said:

"Look at the clock."

They all looked at one another. Then Royal held up the candle and they looked at the tall clock. Its hands pointed to half past three.

Even Eliza Jane did not know what to do. They had waked up Father and Mother, an hour and a half before time to get up.

"What time is it?" Father asked.

Almanzo looked at Royal. Royal and Almanzo looked at Eliza Jane. Eliza Jane swallowed, and opened her mouth, but Alice said:

"Merry Christmas, Father! Merry Christmas, Mother! It's—it's—thirty minutes to four, Father."

Happy holly-day
Holly frames a quaint painting of children departing a country church on this Christmas postcard from 1908.

The clock said, "Tick! Tock! Tick! Tock! Tick!" Then Father chuckled.

Royal opened the dampers of the heater, and Eliza Jane stirred up the kitchen fire and put the kettle on. The house was warm and cosy when Father and Mother got up, and they had a whole hour to spare. There was time to enjoy the presents.

Alice had a gold locket, and Eliza Jane had a pair of garnet earrings. Mother had knitted new lace collars and black lace mitts for them both. Royal had the silk muffler and a fine leather wallet. But Almanzo thought he had the best presents of all. It was a wonderful Christmas.

Then Mother began to hurry, and to hurry everyone else. There were the chores to do, the milk to skim, the new milk to strain and put away, breakfast to eat, vegetables to be peeled, and the whole house must be put in order and everybody dressed up before the company came.

The sun rushed up the sky. Mother was everywhere, talking all the time. "Almanzo, wash your ears! Goodness mercy, Royal, don't stand around underfoot! Eliza Jane, remember you're paring those potatoes, not slicing them, and don't leave so many eyes they can see to jump out of the pot. Count the silver, Alice, and piece it out with the steel knives and forks. The best bleached tablecloths are on the bottom shelf. Mercy on us, look at that clock!"

Sleigh-bells came jingling up the road, and Mother slammed the oven door and ran to change her apron and pin on her brooch; Alice ran downstairs and Eliza Jane ran upstairs, both of them told Almanzo to straighten his collar. Father was calling Mother to fold his cravat. Then Uncle Wesley's sleigh stopped with a last clash of bells.

Almanzo ran out, whooping, and Father and Mother came behind him, as calm as if they had never hurried in their lives. Frank and Fred and Abner and Mary tumbled out of the sleigh, all bundled up, and before Aunt Lindy had handed Mother the baby, Uncle Andrew's sleigh was coming. The yard was full of boys and the house filled with hoopskirts. The uncles stamped snow off their boots and unwound their mufflers.

Royal and Cousin James drove the sleighs into the Buggy-House; they unhitched the horses and put them in stalls and rubbed down their snowy legs.

Almanzo was wearing his boughten cap, and he showed the cousins his jack-knife. Frank's cap was old

Grace
A farm family bows its head in thankfulness for a year's worth of bounty in this Bob Artley cartoon. (Artwork © Bob Artley)

now. He had a jack-knife, but it had only three blades.

Then Almanzo showed his cousins Star and Bright, and the little bobsled, and he let them scratch Lucy's fat white back with corncobs. He said they could look at Starlight if they'd be quiet and not scare him.

The beautiful colt twitched his tail, and came daintily stepping toward them. Then he tossed his head and shied away from Frank's hand thrust through the bars.

"You leave him be!" Almanzo said.

"I bet you don't dast go in there and get on his back," said Frank.

"I dast, but I got better sense," Almanzo told him. "I know better than to spoil that fine colt."

"How'd it spoil him?" Frank said. "Yah, you're scared he'd hurt you! You're scared of that little bitty colt!"

"I am not scared," said Almanzo. "But Father won't let me."

"I guess I'd do it if I wanted to, if I was you. I guess your father wouldn't know," Frank said.

Almanzo didn't answer, and Frank got up on the bars of the stall.

"You get down off there!" Almanzo said, and he took hold of Frank's leg. "Don't you scare that colt!"

"I'll scare him if I want to," Frank said, kicking. Almanzo hung on. Starlight was running around and around the stall, and Almanzo wanted to yell for Royal. But he knew that would frighten Starlight even more.

He set his teeth and gave a mighty tug, and Frank came tumbling down. All the horses jumped, and Starlight reared and smashed against the manger.

"I'll lick you for that," Frank said, scrambling up.

"You just try and lick me!" said Almanzo.

Royal came hurrying from the South Barn. He took Almanzo and Frank by the shoulders and marched them outdoors. Fred and Abner and John came silently after them, and Almanzo's knees wabbled. He was afraid Royal would tell Father.

"Let me catch you boys fooling around those colts again," Royal said, "and I'll tell Father and Uncle Wesley. You'll get the hides thrashed off you."

Royal shook Almanzo so hard that he couldn't tell how hard Royal was shaking Frank. Then he knocked their heads together. Almanzo saw stars.

"Let that teach you to fight. On Christmas Day!

© Sandi Wickersham Resnick

For shame!" Royal said.

"I only didn't want him to scare Starlight," Almanzo said.

"Shut up!" said Royal. "Don't be a tattle-tale. Now you behave yourselves or you'll wish you had. Go wash your hands; it's dinner-time."

They all went into the kitchen and washed their hands. Mother and the aunts and the girl cousins were taking up the Christmas dinner. The dining-table had been turned around and pulled out till it was almost as long as the dining-room, and every inch of it was loaded with good things to eat.

Almanzo bowed his head and shut his eyes tight while Father said the blessing. It was a long blessing, because this was Christmas Day. But at last Almanzo could open his eyes. He sat and silently looked at that table.

He looked at the crisp, crackling little pig lying on the blue platter with an apple in its mouth. He looked at the fat roast goose, the drumsticks sticking up, and the edges of dressing curling out. The sound of Father's knife sharpening on the whetstone made him even hungrier.

He looked at the big bowl of cranberry jelly, and at the fluffy mountain of mashed potatoes with melting butter trickling down it. He looked at the heap of mashed turnips, and the golden baked squash, and the pale fried parsnips.

He swallowed hard and tried not to look anymore. He couldn't help seeing the fried apples'n'onions, and the candied carrots. He couldn't help gazing at the triangles of pie, waiting by his plate; the spicy pumpkin pie, the melting cream pie, the rich, dark mince oozing from between the mince pie's flaky crusts.

He squeezed his hands together between his knees. He had to sit silent and wait, but he felt aching and hollow inside.

All grown-ups at the head of the table must be served first. They were passing their plates, and talking, and heartlessly laughing. The tender pork fell away in slices under Father's carving-knife. The white breast

Classic country Christmas

From making cookies to wrapping gifts, from stockings on the mantel to carolers at the door, Sandi Wickersham captures all the elements in a single, vibrant painting titled "It's Starting to Look a Lot Like Christmas." (Artwork © Sandi Wickersham)

of the goose went piece by piece from the bare breast-bone. Spoons ate up the clear cranberry jelly, and gouged deep into the mashed potatoes, and ladled away the brown gravies.

Almanzo had to wait to the very last. He was youngest of all, except Abner and the babies, and Abner was company.

At last Almanzo's plate was filled. The first taste made a pleasant feeling inside him, and it grew and grew, while he ate and ate and ate. He ate till he could eat no more, and he felt very good inside. For a while he slowly nibbled bits from his second piece of fruit-cake. Then he put the fruity slice in his pocket and went out to play.

Royal and James were choosing sides, to play snow-fort. Royal chose Frank, and James chose Almanzo. When everyone was chosen, they all went to work, rolling snowballs through the deep drifts by the barn. They rolled till the balls were almost as tall as Almanzo; then they rolled them into a wall. They packed snow between them, and made a good fort.

Then each side made its own little snowballs. They breathed on the snow, and squeezed it solid. They made dozens of hard snowballs. When they were ready for the fight, Royal threw a stick into the air and caught it when it came down. James took hold of the stick above Royal's hand, then Royal took hold of it above James' hand, and so on to the end of the stick. James' hand was last, so James' side had the fort.

How the snowballs flew! Almanzo ducked and dodged and yelled, and threw snowballs as fast as he could, till they were all gone. Royal came charging over the wall with all the enemy after him, and Almanzo rose up and grabbed Frank. Headlong they went into the deep snow, outside the wall, and they rolled over and over, hitting each other as hard as they could.

Almanzo's face was covered with snow and his mouth was full of it, but he hung on to Frank and kept hitting him. Frank got him down, but Almanzo squirmed out from under. Frank's head hit his nose, and it began to bleed. Almanzo didn't care. He was on top of Frank, hitting him as hard as he could in the deep snow. He kept saying, "Holler 'nuff! Holler 'nuff!"

Frank grunted and squirmed. He rolled half over, and Almanzo got on top of him. He couldn't stay on top of Frank and hit him, so he bore down with all his weight, and he pushed Frank's face deeper and deeper into the snow. And Frank gasped: "'Nuff!"

Almanzo got up on his knees, and he saw Mother in the doorway of the house. She called:

"Boys! Boys! Stop playing now. It's time to come in and warm."

They were warm. They were hot and panting. But Mother and the aunts thought the cousins must get warm before they rode home in the cold. They all went tramping in, covered with snow, and Mother held up her hands and exclaimed:

"Mercy on us!"

The grown-ups were in the parlor, but the boys had to stay in the dining-room, so they wouldn't melt on the parlor carpet. They couldn't sit down, because the chairs were covered with blankets and laprobes, warming by the heater. But they ate apples and drank cider, standing around, and Almanzo and Abner went into the pantry and ate bits off the platters.

Then uncles and aunts and the girl cousins put on their wraps, and they brought the sleeping babies from the bedroom, rolled up in shawls. The sleighs came jingling from the barn, and Father and Mother helped tuck in the blankets and laprobes, over the hoopskirts. Everybody called: "Good-by! Good-by!"

The music of the sleigh-bells came back for a little while; then it was gone. Christmas was over.

Next stop, the table
Now that the goose is ready for the serving platter, Christmas dinner can begin. (Photograph © J. C. Allen & Son)

Not just for kids

Right: *Children aren't the only ones who enjoy fresh air and winter outdoor activities. Outdoor activities give adults a chance to work up an appetite for the big holiday feast—or work off its aftereffects. (Photographs © J. C. Allen & Son)*

Winter sports

Above and right: *Who wants to be cooped up inside when there are snowy hillsides and frozen ponds to be conquered? Christmas, of course, means a vacation from school, leaving children with whole days free for sledding, ice skating, snowball fights, snowman building, and other winter sports.* (Photographs © J. C. Allen & Son)

Christmas at Route 1, Box 111, Aurora

By Shirley Schoonover

The memories of childhood have no order at all but come lilting and spilling like the snows of all those winters," says writer Shirley Schoonover. Just as her memories come lilting and spilling, so do her words. Her language and descriptions are as breathless, sprawling, exuberant, and energetic as the child she describes herself to be.

The daughter of Finnish farmers, Schoonover grew up on a farm on the Iron Range of northern Minnesota and was educated at the University of Minnesota and the University of Nebraska. She is a novelist and short story writer whose talent has earned her two O. Henry awards.

This account of Christmases on the farm are part of the rush of childhood memories Schoonover captured in her essay "Route 1, Box 222, Aurora," which can be found in the anthology *Growing Up in Minnesota: Ten Writers Remember Their Childhoods* (1976).

Holstein holiday
Cows will certainly join in a farm's Christmas celebration, as long as gratuitous manger references are kept to a minimum. (Photograph © Lynn Stone)

WITH WINTER, OF course, there was Christmas. The Christmas I remember most was when we ate Petrice, our goose. She had come to our farm as a gosling. Thinking she was a gander, we named her Pete. When she laid an egg, we renamed her Petrice. She thought she was human and would have nothing to do with the other fowl. She always followed me around the farm, daffy, crooning to me, and I could never sit down without her getting into my lap and resting her head on my neck. She also wanted to mother puppies, and when our cocker bitch, Flicka, left her babes unattended once, Petrice nestled on them, wings outspread, crazy eyes soft and maternal. What a hooha there was when Flicka discovered Petrice gabbling there. The puppies didn't mind, but Flicka went mad. Foaming at the mouth, she attacked. Petrice did her best to fly, but, weighing twenty pounds, all she could do was lollop away, flapping her wings, while Flicka helped her along by grabbing mouthfuls of rump and feathers. Around and around the house they went, Petrice trundling, lurching, and honking and Flicka snapping and spitting out feathers. At last, poor Petrice ran headlong for the doghouse and stuck fast in the doorway, her fanny exposed, her cries dreadful, as Flicka lay down and promptly began denuding that plump backside. I scolded Flicka away and pityingly hauled Petrice feetfirst out of the doghouse. And when Christmas came and Petrice lay wreathed with parsley on the platter, I could not touch a drumstick or lay a fork on her white meat. I could not eat at all; cranberry sauce sparkled, sweet potatoes swam in golden sauce, apple pie bubbled and crisped, all to no avail, as I sat, pea green, at the table, poised on the edge of my chair, the brittle tears ready to break down my face.

But that was the only sad Christmas. All the other Christmases roll together into a white and woolly ball of remembering how it was to come to the rim of wakefulness on Christmas morning and lie there quilted and snug before flying out of bed to see what magic had happened during the night. There were always two kinds of presents. The practical kind included long woolen underpants and vests, always from an aunt who didn't know my size and so made them big enough to fit a cow, and knitted socks and caps that were too small, and a handmade pink satin brassiere trimmed with tatted roses from one of my daffier aunts, and the hated long cotton stockings with new suspenders from Santa Claus (my mother's handwriting), two suits of long underwear with trapdoors in back, and flannel pajamas to guarantee I'd never freeze at night, especially since I slept in my underwear. But the presents I liked were naturally not practical or useful to anyone but a child: candy canes and gumballs, red-and-green-striped ribbon candy, and a paper sack of orange bubble gum and licorice drops, once a gun that shot rubber-tipped darts with a real imitation leather holster, a whistle that made the dogs bark, a celluloid doll who wet profusely when fed (when she broke her head I used her to scoop snow cones), a bag of balloons, wax fangs that fit over my teeth. And a small blackboard with chalk, which was best of all, for in secret I practiced writing every dirty word I knew, only I was found out and got treated to another sitting spell behind the kitchen stove.

And then it was breakfast of oatmeal, which I dabbled at, mouth full of ribbon candy, hands sticky from sorting through the gumballs and candy canes. Then prinked and combed and stuffed into my blue rayon satin dress and tight black shoes, coated, hatted, and off to the Palo Congregational Church to discreetly suck on gumballs and pop tiny bubbles until my mother caught me and gave me such a pinch that I swallowed the gum.

Home from church, the long Christmas day spread out before us with aunts, uncles, and cousins coming by to kiss under the mistletoe. "Slobbering," I called it. All red-checked and smelling of Christmas colognes and after-shave lotion. There were the giddy, older girl cousins from Markham parading their fiancés and gaudy engagement rings while the spinsters whispered in the kitchen, "She *has* to, you know!" The uncles and my father would step out to the barn to look at the cows and to wet their whistles with a pre-dinner drink of Old Crow. The aunts and my mother tacked back and forth setting the long damasked table, carrying platters and bowls, scattering silver, folding napkins, unmolding the jello salad, basting the turkey, and hitting the head of whichever child got caught jam-handed or pickle-fingered.

Dinner was called and we all tucked in, barely

Almost ready

The aroma of the holiday turkey draws the whole family to the farm kitchen. Preparations for a Christmas meal often begin days, even weeks, before the table is set. (Photograph © J. C. Allen & Son)

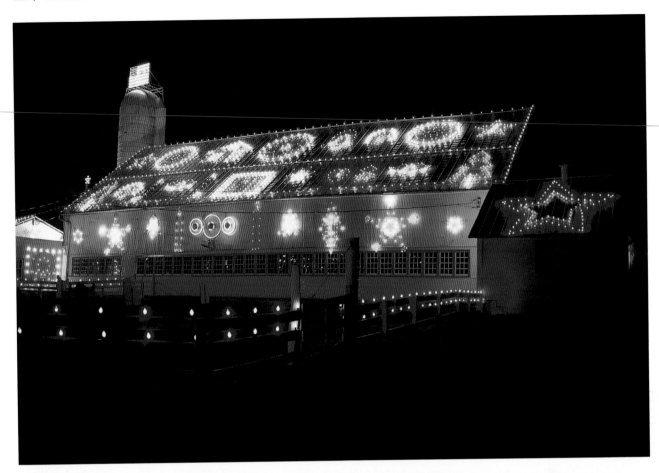

"Drumstick, please"
Right: *It pays to be specific when it comes to turkey, as this young girl knows. (Photograph © J. C. Allen & Son)*

Impressive illumination
Facing page, both photos: *Sometimes a wreath just isn't enough. A barn as big as this one in Pennsylvania calls for an impressive display of illumination. (Photographs © Keith Baum)*

waiting for manners; the plates were passed to my father, who laid on slices of turkey and handed the plates to my mother, who piled on mashed potatoes and ladled gravy, while aunts forked over the pickles, watermelon and dill, the walnut stuffing, and the vegetables, and we children lavished jellies and jam over our biscuits. We all ate beyond the bursting point and then begged for dessert: mince pies, marble cakes, raisin and cherry tarts, plum pudding, fruit-filled cookies, and chocolate candies—until one or another child turned pale and had to be led outdoors to be sick in the snow.

After dinner, the uncles and my father loosened their belts and shoelaces, belching behind polite hands, lighting their pipes and cigarettes, feet up, talking heavily and slowly, sometimes nodding into a doze. The aunts and my mother, elbows deep in soapsuds,

coffee cups within reach, gossiped and creaked within their corsets and girdles. We children, adrift without a single parental eye tracking us, would sneak out to spy on the courting couples and snigger and simper in mockery at such moonstruck goonery, and if we caught them kissing we would smack our lips at them and howl like devils until some enraged swain came bangfooting after us, murderous and lusting for our blood.

But then the roistering day must end; the Christmas candles sputtered out, and the heavy twilight was now lanterned by the headlights of departing aunts and uncles and drowsing cousins. Then I sat in the starry tinseled Christmas glow and watched the snowflakes swaddling the earth anew with a white and silent light as the humming, holy night closed around me.

Recipe for Christmas

By Robert P. T. Coffin

Robert P. T. Coffin is a poet, essayist, artist, teacher, and New Englander. He is the author of more than three dozen works of prose, poetry, and history, many of which he illustrated himself. In 1936, he was awarded a Pulitzer Prize for his book of verse *Strange Holiness*. Born in Brunswick, Maine, he was educated at Bowdoin College, Princeton, and Oxford. He eventually returned to Bowdoin College as a professor of English.

One of Coffin's favorite topics is his boyhood on Lost Paradise, the saltwater farm on which he grew up. "I began being a poet . . . among lighthouses and barns and boats, tides and fogs and apples and hired men, on that best kind of farm," he writes with pride. His writing sparkles with his enthusiasm and affection for farm life. When reading his words, one can almost see his eyes light up as he remembers the Christmases of his youth.

"Recipe for Christmas" is one of the essays collected in Coffin's 1944 book *Mainstays of Maine*.

Community Christmas
In Hebron, New Hampshire, a community gazebo sparkles with holiday lights and trimmings. (Photograph © William Johnson)

THERE ARE ALL kinds of Christmases, I know. But my recipe for that feast is the only one I have found that has no flaws in it. It is the kind of Christmas I had as a boy, under Misery Hill in Harpswell, Maine, on Lost Paradise Farm.

The items that go into the making of this holiday are fairly common ones. But they must be exactly as I describe them and put together just so.

You must have a farm, first of all. I have heard of a Christmas without a farm, but it was a rather quiet affair and didn't send out many sparks. Now I am the last person in the world to be fussy about things, but the farm must absolutely be a saltwater one. There have been Christmases without the ocean, as there were once Christmases without bells. But I notice that the ballad makers always mixed the sea and church bells right in with the first Christmas of all:

Joseph did whistle and Mary did sing,
—Mary did sing, Mary did sing,
And all the bells on earth did ring
For joy our Lord was born.

O they sail'd in to Bethlehem!
—To Bethlehem, to Bethlehem;
Saint Michael was the steresman,
Saint John sate in the horn.

Yes, you must have the ocean. All good farms, of course, are small ones, and what is more, small New England ones. And of these eligible northern New England ones, only the Maine ones count. But the only Maine ones worth looking at twice are the saltwater farms. And the sole saltwater farms worth their salt are the ones on Casco Bay, or more particularly on my Great Island in Casco Bay. As I say, I don't like to be fussy, but that's how it stands in my recipe!

All right. Say you've got your farm, on Great Island, and one with the ocean on two sides of it, like mine. Then you need a good cold snap, with the stars sputtering in the sky, and you freeze the ocean so hard that your father, coming from town, can drive his horse-sled right over it, and you can skate out to meet him, the night before Christmas Eve, with the farm lantern. You hold the lantern up for him, and he comes into the light in his great buffalo-robe coat with his breath around him like a halo and long icicles tinkling on his wide moustache.

As I keep saying, I like to be open-minded about things. But unless you can produce a father exactly like mine, it will probably be no use going on with your Christmas pudding. My father was a good singer, a fine story-teller, a man who was still over half boy, and he made me think of the starry sky when I looked at him in the eyes. He was also a good gunner, and would take time to go gunning right in the middle of a bag of russets he was picking. If you have that kind of a father, it's right. You can go on getting ready for Christmas.

You've got to have snow, of course, a pretty good fall of it. So you can see the lacework of rabbit tracks and mice tracks wherever you go in the woods. You must go into the woods the day before Christmas. For there will be the tree to cut. Now this is absolutely essential: You must cut that tree yourself. You must use your judgment as to the right one. It is conceivable that a Christmas might be a Christmas with a tree somebody else cut, but it would be a pretty slim and pindling one. You take your father's best axe, almost as long as you are, and you go out into the woods alone, holding the axe over your shoulder at the balance, the way a man carries his. You may have to walk a mile or two to shake off some of your more adhesive small brothers, but it must be done. This is a one-man job. You scare up a partridge, and he fills the clean air with powdered diamonds as he goes up through the trees. For of course the sun is out brilliant, and the boughs are sparkling with snow on every twig. The tree you want, of course, is a fir. If your farm is like my Lost Paradise one, you will have about three thousand to pick from. You will come on a perfect fir tree at last, with its branches even all around. But you will never think of cutting that one down. That would spoil your whole Christmas. You are a New Englander, and you must never use the best you have, common. You must not destroy a pattern of the perfect. You go on till you find a fir not quite perfection. It must be one that is just the right height to tip the sitting-room ceiling and no more. For the top plume must never be bent over. You cut the lower boughs off, and you bring it down with two hacks on each side. Then you catch the tree at the balance and start home. You walk in the middle of your fir, with a fragrant cloud of spicy boughs up level with your eyes. You saw the butt off even in the woodshed, and nail the standards on yourself. Then you take the tree into the house and set it up. Your mother leaves a mince pie right in the air, to come and see and applaud.

The night before Christmas
" 'Twas the night before Christmas and all through the house not a creature was stirring, not even a mouse. . . ." A grandmother shares a warm, quiet moment with her grandchildren. (Photograph © J. C. Allen & Son)

That reminds me: You must have a mother as nearly like mine as mothers come. That is, she must be one who makes good mince pies—and apple, squash, blueberry, huckleberry, custard, and lemon—helps you with your sums with one arm while she rocks the baby to sleep with the other and sings him a lullaby in the midst of the multiplication table, and look very beautiful.

The mother is very useful at Christmas. For she strings the popcorn—after popping it—cuts out the colored paper links you paste together in chains for the tree, and makes up the popcorn balls out of molasses and hot butter. She also cooks the goose, twenty-five pumpkin pies, three steamed puddings, and roasts the three roosters that make up the edging for the colossal Christmas dinner for the family clan. She has started the mincemeat and the Christmas puddings off to ripen back two months ago. And the jellies and jams and preserves on the table she started, many jars

of them, before you were born. The sunlight of the past twenty years on this saltwater farm she has saved under glass along her cellar shelves.

The goose, naturally, is the center of Christmas. I once knew a farmer family that had a turkey for the center, but it was a family that was small potatoes and few in a hill, they did not get on in the world very far. I think they ended up snuffing ashes in the city. The goose, by the way, must be one you have mashed up turnips for these past four months, and he must weigh at least twelve pounds.

Before I forget it, you had better mix into your Christmas dish about four brothers and five sisters. Otherwise you won't have the kind of Christmas that is correct. I don't like to be constantly insisting on things, but the brothers had better be all as different as night and day, some carpenters in short pants, some preachers, some masons, some students, and as cranky and conceited and generous as my brothers were. And

Nautical flair
Above: *Braided rope gives this wreath a nautical flair, appropriate for the door of any coastal farmhouse. (Photograph © Leslie M. Newman)*

Coastal Christmas
Right: *Artist Sandi Wickersham obviously relishes the idea of a holiday on a coastal farm as much as writer Robert P. T. Coffin. Her enthusiasm is apparent in her painting "Dog Days of Winter." (Artwork © Sandi Wickersham)*

when it comes to the sisters, you better be sure they are all quite different, too, and full of spice and genius for cutting out paperdolls and sewing you up in your best corduroy pants so your mother will not see the three-cornered tear you got in them when you hung yourself up, like Absalom, on the beams in the barn.

Oh, yes, and cousins. These are especially important. They are sort of lumber out of which you will build your house of mirth Christmas Day. They are much more pliable than brothers, and you can afford to cut to waste, with them. I don't know how it is with other large families, but mine could never act along at Christmas time unless there were, say, two full platoons of he- and she-cousins to come over the ice of

the bays from the four points of the compass, by sleds, by skates, by shank's mare, to break my new music-box's heart by too much cranking, to fight with me and slide with me, and eat too many of the cornballs with spills stuck to them from their contact with the Christmas tree's boughs. And they all went home worn out but contented, full of goose and apple dumplings, and fell asleep standing up and had to be undressed like so many three-year-olds and put to bed to rest up for another Christmas.

Cousins mean uncles. These should decidedly be like mine. Some with long beards and gates-ajar moustaches, some lazy and fond of sleep, and so good cushions for a nine-year-old boy to sit on and read, and some who carve you out ships from white pine and

©Sandi Wickersham Resnick

rig them up to the last royals with horsehair and cotton cloth and glue. Some of them should go sliding with you, by all means, and snag their Sunday-go-to-meeting trousers on stumps and come home as dishevelled as you are, to keep you company.

Aunts, too. They can help with the carving and singing, and crack the walnuts. And all talk at once till the house sings like a beehive in the month of June.

And one aunt should be on hand there the night before Christmas, ahead of the rest, to read the Christmas story in Luke. And after she has finished it, you must get your pail and go right out into the middle of the story she has been reading, and feed the calves and milk your string of cows. This is the only proper beginning to Christmas Eve. You sit there quiet in the dusk and lean your head in on the cow's warm side and smell the hay and hear all the cuds being chewed in harmony, and you yourself make sounds like little bells of Christmas as you squirt the milk into the tin pail between your knees. The barn smells like Christmas. The cows fill it with their sweet breath. The snow lights up in the lantern light along the window sashes of the tie-up. You get to feeling the door might open any minute to the outside and let you see a host of angels singing and coming down along the cold sky of Casco Bay right to Great Island.

And wood, remember, is a good part of a farm Christmas. You fetch that, too, for your older brothers are too near being men, being twelve or so, to stoop to such work. You are the man to keep the fireplace fed. So you carry in beech and birch and spruce till you start the after seam of your breeches. You take in Maine Summer hardened into wood. And last year's sunlight comes rippling out of the fireplace and lights up the sitting-room for the tree's trimming.

You trim the tree yourselves, you brothers and sisters, the night before Christmas. You take turns at it, with all the rest handing you things and holding the baby's highchair as you make the festoons fast. The main principle to go on is to hang the popcorn and paper strings in loops from every twig and put a big red apple on at every place the loops touch the tree. You tie the candles on last. Real candles that can be lit tomorrow night.

You go to bed at last. That is, you make believe go. For one by one, all you brothers and sisters, steal down to hang your presents to the others, in deadly secret, on the tree. You coincide and collide, of course, on the stairs and among the branches of the tree, in a room full of shadows, now that the embers have burned low. But collisions are expected. You get back into bed at length. Your window should be a dormer one, like mine. You vow you will lie awake and watch the stars and wonder about what is in the long package with your name on it below stairs. And suddenly it is broad daylight, and the house is reeling with Apache yells. You go down with your breeches on only one leg and join in the riot under the tree. You take your presents down and look at them. But—such is the law in this Christmas of mine—you have to hang them all back. Presents, of course, come in all kinds. But unless you have a popgun with a barrel striped like a broomstick, it won't really be Christmas for you. And a top that sings a sweet tune as it stands still on one place and spins like a good fellow. And a Noah's ark for a smaller brother, that your father has made the world's stripedest zebras for, and best elephants, and you wish you were only half as tall as you are and could own the whole business yourself.

After an aeon or two you are dragged to breakfast by older members of the family. You finish your flapjacks and molasses just in the nick. The uncles and aunts and cousins begin to blow in. The house becomes too small. All the wearers of trousers, from three-year-olds to eighty-yearers, and most of the wearers of skirts, overflow upon the white hillsides and into the woods, to work up an appetite. The farm dog takes up the trail of a rabbit. Guns crack. Partridges boom. Small boys and girls catapult down the hills and out across the bay, and

Country cousins
No Christmas is complete without cousins, and the best cousins are the ones that come bearing gifts and toys to share. (Photograph © J. C. Allen & Son)

Rhode Island fields
Snow-swept fields surround a Victorian farm in Rhode Island. (Photograph © Paul Rezendes)

go halfway across to Spain. Boys with barrel staves for skis turn bottoms up in the sunlight. All the older people crowd into the pung and horse-sled and go up and down the bay with great clanging of bells. Some boys start a bonfire in the woods, but the snow is deep enough to keep the farm from going up in smoke.

But everyone converges on the farmhouse at two. Then all hands sit down to the goose, the roosters, and puddings and pies. Some of the smaller fry may founder here, for boys' eyes are notoriously bigger than their bellies.

The sun goes down while the eating is still going on, and the pine shadows come into the windows from the west. Small boys fall asleep with their faces in their plates. Lamps come out. Candles are lighted. The tree comes ablaze. One uncle is told off to put out the boughs that catch afire from the guttering tree lights. The presents come down for good. Then you all sing carols to the tune of the parlor melodeon, which an aunt plays in the parlor in the air of Greenland and in

danger of pneumonia while you sit in the Summer from the hearth and let your voices out. Uncles and aunts with young babies leave from time to time. But the ranks are closed up, and the singing goes on. When all the voices are used up, your father, who has held himself in reserve, starts a story. You get down on your full belly and listen, watching the bright tides that ebb and flow in the golden coals. Your father's voice goes farther and farther away. It is across the ocean at last. And then it is close, and he is helping you up the stairs to your bed and the starry window above. You fall like a log, and you go miles down too deep for dreams, weighed down with raisins and goose.

And one more Christmas is over on Lost Paradise Farm.

I envy all of you who can work up such another Christmas from this recipe of mine this year. And Merry Christmas to you all!

Chapter 5

Memories of a Christmas Past

"It has been a surprise to me to discover that most of my own memories of Christmas are not of big family gatherings or great spreads of presents. More often memory is triggered by something small."
—Ben Logan, *Christmas Remembered*

Sometimes there is one particular Christmas that makes an impact and sticks in a child's mind. Perhaps it involved a long-wished-for present, an extraordinary event, the beginning of a family tradition, or a subtle lesson learned. Be it big or small, that memory stays clear and frozen forever. It lingers in the back of the mind, resurfacing again and again as years go by.

In this chapter, three writers share their particular special Christmas memory.

Sleigh bells
The past meets the present in Bill Breedon's "Sleigh Bells, Too." Although this setting is the present, the architecture and atmosphere of the country village evoke warm memories of times gone by. (Artwork © 1999 Bill Breedon/Applejack Licensing)

All the Difference in the World

by Dan Jorgensen

Part of growing up is the realization that there is more to Christmas than gifts, Santa Claus, massive feasts, and visiting families. And for many children, one Christmas often brings the deeper meanings of the holiday into crisp focus.

For writer Dan Jorgensen, it was the Christmas when he was ten years old, when the traditional Christmas Eve pageant held in his one-room schoolhouse sparked his appreciation for the "neighborhood" of which his family was a part in rural South Dakota.

"On the farm, a neighbor is someone who stands ready to assist you on a moment's notice, in good times and bad," he says. That spirit of community is the strongest value Jorgensen took away from his childhood on the farm and from the Christmas of 1957.

Jorgensen's writing career has spanned more than thirty years. It includes five novels (four for young adults) and myriad stories penned for newspapers in his former home state of South Dakota and his current home state of Minnesota. He continues to pursue fiction writing, while his weekly column "Jargon," a gentle-humored look at American life, appears in a dozen Minnesota and South Dakota newspapers.

Waiting, wishing
Many a child has tried to stay awake on Christmas Eve, waiting to hear the sound of reindeer hooves on the roof and Santa Claus's laugh as he lands on the hearth. (Photograph © J. C. Allen & Son)

THE EXPERIENCE OF a Christmas pageant in our country school was one I had each and every year. Yet it is one particular pageant—one done in 1957, when I was ten years old—that sticks most clearly in my mind.

It wasn't because of any special role that I played, although I do remember having graduated from being just a shepherd to the much more important part of a wise man. No, it was something much richer and fuller than that. That particular Christmas pageant was the first time I really stopped to think about the adults around me and the "parts" they were playing in the mini-pageant that made up my own life.

I grew up on a South Dakota farm in the 1950s. Planted in the heart of this little world in which we resided was our one-room, wood-frame school house, and like the other country schools that served many parts of America in those years, it was a picture of efficiency. Our teacher, a pinch-nosed, thin-haired, slightly overweight man named Mr. Glanzer, took care of all eight grades and had us neatly organized row-by-row with the littlest kids directly in front of his big desk on through the seventh and eighth graders occupying the back.

Mr. Glanzer had come to our school from somewhere "back East." He moved around from farm to farm during the school year, and we never really found out where he disappeared to in the summer months. He had been there for half-a-dozen years by the time I started school, and he was still there when I moved on to high school in the early 1960s.

School began after the hay harvest was in, during the sweltering dog days of late summer and early fall. Our school was poorly insulated and thus "heated up nicely" during those days. Likewise, when the colder fall weather and winter arrived, it "cooled down" just as fast. While we had a coal-burning furnace in the school basement, Mr. Glanzer tried to stay ahead of the cold by setting up a pot-bellied stove in the back of the room.

The installation of the pot-bellied stove, usually done around the first week of November, signaled that we soon would have the chance to do even more to alter the appearance of our one-room school. We'd never know for sure when the momentous day would come, but somewhere around the third week of November, Mr. Glanzer would solemnly stop classes and announce, "Well, children, it's time. It's time to build the stage."

Building the stage meant two things: Christmas was not far away, and it was time for us to start preparing for our annual Christmas pageant.

One of the traditions Mr. Glanzer had brought with him was that pageant. He had labored long and hard to get the idea together and approved by the school board, and by the time I reached fifth grade it was, indeed, a tradition in the school district.

To help Mr. Glanzer with his grand scheme, he had enlisted the farm fathers to help him construct the stage. The farmers had joined together to cut planks and build a platform that went across nearly the entire front of the room and took up a full one-fourth of the space. For it to work properly, Mr. Glanzer had to move his desk in among his students for a four or five-week period.

"Building" the stage for us really meant putting it back together. Under Mr. Glanzer's watchful eye and based on his plan, the stage had first been constructed much like a large Lego set. Each piece was neatly fit into the other. To rebuild it each year, the oldest boys carried the base blocks and put them in place.

The school's youngest girl was responsible for cleaning off Baby Jesus' manger and filling it with fresh straw that Mr. Glanzer acquired. "Good looking straw," he'd say to one or another of the farmers with whom he'd be boarding—usually staring at the strawstack created by the threshing machine. The farmer or his wife would immediately know that Mr. Glanzer wanted some of that straw for the Christmas pageant, and they would usually deliver it to the school that same week. What wasn't used in the manger was spread on the floor nearby to put the final touch on the manger scene.

Since it was nearly impossible to put up a curtain, several donated sheets and blankets were strung up on the front right and left corners of the stage, tied to nails protruding from the ceiling. These covered just enough of the stage to give us the chance to be off stage and out of sight when we weren't performing. (These worked just fine unless you forgot which side you were supposed to go off before preparing for your next scene, thus creating comic relief where it wasn't actually intended.)

In the first week after our stage was in place, Mr. Glanzer went about the business of casting both the Christmas story and all the other pieces. The Christmas pageant, to be sure, was the retelling of the story

Weathered barn
Having already survived many harsh mountain winters, this weathered barn still manages to hang on for just one more season. (Photograph © Scott T. Smith)

of Christ's birth story—something condoned in public schools during those more innocent times. In our version, the oldest boy and oldest girl got to play Mary and Joseph, with the youngest first graders being either the "star" or the "angel." Usually the triumphs and disappointments associated with deciding who got what roles would be offset by Mr. Glanzer's judicious selection of those other little Christmas-related play pieces, thus giving each and every student the chance to say lines or sing a solo or duet on the pageant night.

Mr. Glanzer managed to teach us the songs to be performed on pageant night and set up ways for us to practice our lines while still not taking away from a regular class schedule. Because of his planning expertise, we always seemed to end up with an hour at the end of each day to work on the pageant, finalizing

©Sandi Wickersham Resnick

our lines and entrance and exit cues, and doing any final decorating touches to make the entire school-room as Christmasy as possible.

The year I was ten years old, staring out at the happy, expectant faces of those farm families who were watching us perform, I realized, for the first time, that participating in the Christmas pageant meant more than just tromping across that rough-hewn stage and having a good time. I realized that I was part of a community, and that what I was doing meant something special to someone else. Our pageant brought everyone in the area—all of our parents, grandparents, aunts, uncles and even city cousins—together in a community reunion. Nothing else, not even harvests, did as much.

For the first time in my young life, I remember feeling a strange lump forming in my throat as we kids stood at the center of that stage singing "Silent Night" at evening's end.

The shock of seeing tears streaming down my mother's face was only compounded when I saw tears on the normally placid face of Mr. Glanzer. At that moment, it also dawned on me then that our community was more than just a place for him to work. It was, in fact, his community, too, and his pride in what "his kids" were accomplishing meant just as much to him as it did to their proud parents sitting in the audience.

I have a photograph taken in front of our school my fifth grade year with all twenty-three students gathered on the front step, Mr. Glanzer standing sternly in our midst. While there's little resemblance by him to either Santa Claus or any other personification of Christmas, he did indeed represent the true spirit of Christmas. Because, what he brought with him to our farm community—his community by adoption—enhanced each and every person's Christmas season and expanded our lives. The pageant was his Christmas gift to us, a gift that ultimately made all the difference in the world.

Winter memories

Among the plethora of winter memories depicted in this painting by Sandi Wickersham is a young girl with blonde pigtails and a black Labrador retriever. The Lab is her childhood companion Coalie and the pigtailed girl is Wickersham herself as a child. The two friends continue to play together, because Wickersham includes them both in every painting she creates. (Artwork © Sandi Wickersham)

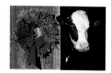

Toys from Dad's Workshop

By Bob Artley

Farm country life has supplied a lifetime of inspiration for cartoonist and writer Bob Artley. With a deft pen and warm sense of humor, he fondly remembers the animals, equipment, chores, seasons, and events—both everyday and extraordinary—that made up his boyhood on a farm in Hampton, Iowa.

Artley began his career as an editorial cartoonist for the *Des Moines Tribune* and continued it at the Worthington *Daily Globe* in western Minnesota. He also worked in advertising and, in partnership with his wife Ginny, was the publisher of two weekly newspapers. Now retired, he continues to write, draw, and paint at his farm in Iowa—the same farm on which he grew up and which has been in his family for more than a century.

His artwork and writings have been collected into a number of books, including *Country Christmas: As Remembered By a Former Kid* (1994), from which the following selection was taken. His special Christmas memory of the gifts from his father's workshop pays homage to the resourcefulness and creativity that Christmas brings out in farm parents everywhere.

Surprise!
For grade-school-age youngsters, Christmas morning just can't come fast enough. It is difficult to sleep when there are presents to open and new toys to discover, and the excitement propels children out of bed before the sun comes up. (Photograph © J. C. Allen & Son)

DURING MOST OF the year, my brothers and I had access to Dad's workshop where we were free to experiment in our crude attempts at making things. A few weeks before Christmas, however, this fascinating place became closed to us.

After the chores were done and supper was over Dad would put on his barn jacket and cap and disappear for the evening to his workshop. Sometimes Mom would join him while we kids, burning with curiosity and excitement, tried to occupy ourselves as best we could until Mom returned, aglow with some Christmas secret she and Dad shared.

From our upstairs bedroom we could see the yellow light of Dad's kerosene lantern shining from the workshop window. Thus, after Mom had tucked us in for the night, we were all set for pleasant dreams.

No mansion or palace, with its many spendered trappings of the season, could have offered more of the spirit and magic of Christmas than we, as children, experienced in the frugal surroundings of our farm home. Those years, I was to learn later, were a period of financial hard times. There was barely enough money to pay for the necessities, let alone to indulge in extravagant giving that, even then, was becoming the vogue. We kids didn't know that, however. Isolated as we were on a little-used road of dirt (or mud, much of the year), our contacts were mostly with those in similar circumstances. We felt rich.

Even pouring over the magazines and mail-order catalogs that came and seeing their illustrations of well-formed and lavishly decorated Christmas trees, with attractively wrapped gifts piled high beneath, only added to our enjoyment of the season. In no way did it detract from the appreciation we felt for our own spindly tree, with its meager, mostly homemade decorations, and the modest pile of gifts beneath.

Most often these gifts were of a practical nature, clothing or books. A few inexpensive toys or games would be found too, wrapped in brightly colored or white tissue paper and placed beneath the tree or among the fragrant pine boughs. I will not forget the happy Christmas we found a wind-up train on an oval track among the wrapped packages beneath the decorated tree.

But what made Christmases so extra special for us kids were the toys that came from Dad's workshop. Along with the wonderful fragrance of evergreen boughs, the scent of freshly worked pine and new paint (barely dry) is one that will forever bring to mind those magical Christmases of my youth.

The first toy I remember coming from Dad's workshop was a little red barn, complete with fences and cut-out wooden horses, cows, and pigs. I must have been two years old that Christmas. Dad played with me on the floor showing me how to set up the fences and put the cows in their stanchions and the horses in their stalls.

The next Christmas Dad made a wooden pull-toy dog, jointed so that it waggled when pulled. This toy was mostly for Dean who was a little over one year old at the time. As I recall, Dad made several of these toys, which were given to some of our small cousins and friends.

A little table and two chairs came from Dad's shop the Christmas I was four and Dean was two. The bright red paint was barely dry Christmas morning and permeated the house with a new-paint smell. This small-size furniture was not only fun but practical as well and was used much by my brothers and me and by our small cousins and friends when they came to visit. Down through the years, after much use, repairs, and repainting they have always remained "the little red table and chairs."

No farm is complete without a farmhouse. I must have been five the Christmas a toy house and a windmill came out of Dad's shop to join the little barn. Mom had made curtains to hang from the one window. Inside the little house was a store-bought cast-iron range. With it came an iron pot and skillet and an iron lifter that really worked for taking off the little stove lids. Also bought for the little house was a table and chair set stamped out of lithographed tin.

Under the little wooden windmill, with a wheel that turned in the wind, was a tiny iron pump. By working the little handle up and down, one could really pump water from and back into a small iron tank at its base.

In October, for his fifth birthday, Dean was given

Historical charm

Antique American toys—from dolls to teddy bears, a rocking horse to a board game—give this country Christmas tree a historical charm. (Photograph © Daniel Dempster)

a toy locomotive made of heavy gauge metal. We both enjoyed playing with this toy, for it reflected our interest in the freight trains that daily passed through our neighborhood.

That year, as in other years, there was the pain of anticipation and the fun of trying to guess what it was that Dad was making for us for Christmas. We heard the sounds of sawing, hammering, and sanding coming from the workshop. Both our parents teased us by giving us clues as to what the big secret was. They hinted that it was black and red and about six feet long. How we puzzled over that bit of information!

Then one day, shortly before Christmas, we were stopped at a railroad crossing waiting for a string of freight cars to pass. Mom called Dad's attention to a freshly painted boxcar passing before us. It was only after Christmas morning that Mom's seemingly innocent observation and Dad's acknowledgment of it had meaning for us.

The sight that greeted us that Christmas morning was one that would delight any child. Three wooden train cars, reeking of new paint and coupled to the familiar metal toy locomotive, almost dwarfed the Christmas tree and the meager supply of packages beneath. Dad had turned out a bright red boxcar, a black coal car or gondola, and a caboose, also a bright red.

We spent many gleeful moments that day, not only examining and playing with the train, but also confronting our parents concerning the ambiguous clues with which they had teased us as the train was secretly being made in Dad's shop.

Most of the toys Dad made for us were just that, toys. They were not miniature scale models of the real thing. The last toy to come out of Dad's shop for Dean and me, however, was a little haystacker that really worked, in its own small way.

As we pulled the string over two small pulleys (which Dad had made by cutting down a couple of empty spools from Mom's sewing basket) the little stacker would lift a small bunch of cut grass and deposit it in a pile that was soon a little haystack. This activity, of course, had to wait until summer.

White Christmas
Nestled in the snowy Wasatch Mountains of Utah, a dairy farm displays its Christmas cheer with a wreath on the barn. (Photograph © Scott T. Smith)

More workshop gifts

Dad wasn't the only resourceful one in Bob Artley's family. With a little ingenuity and handiwork, anyone could create a gift in the farm workshop. (Artwork © Bob Artley)

As the years passed and Dean and I grew older, Dad no longer made gifts for us. We had graduated to things like air rifles and skis. And, of course, books and clothes were still appreciated. But we did enjoy being in on the secrets watching the progress of the toys Dad continued to make for our younger brother and cousins.

The Christmas after Dan had turned six or seven, Dad made him a whole set of little farm buildings, including a house, barn, silo, hog house, corn crib, and machine shed. There were also some small village buildings: a church, depot, and general store. The round silo was carved from the limb of an ash tree. It had a domed roof and was painted to look like a clay block silo.

Dan and his playmates enjoyed these toys as much as Dean and I had ours. But he took better care of his and kept them for his children and now his grandchildren to enjoy.

I wish we still had the little farm building that Dad made for Dean and me. We would care for them as valued relics of our childhood. But, sad to say, the little house, barn, and windmill, much like their full-scale counterparts across the country, have disintegrated back into the earth from which they came. These toys, as well as others Dad made for us, have become a part of the soil beneath the shade of maples where we so often played with them.

I suppose it is only in the maturity of our latter years that we value the artifacts of our lives as objects of historical value or treasured keepsakes. In hindsight I cannot imagine why we didn't take better care of those heirlooms, which they certainly were. But as children we did value them highly as toys to use and to enjoy for that brief moment of childhood.

Something for everyone

Above: *After the long wait, Christmas Day has finally arrived, and there is something for everyone beneath the tree. With this many wonderful toys, the key lesson this Christmas undoubtedly will be about learning to share. (Photograph © J. C. Allen & Son)*

Heigh-ho!

Left: *Few people know that long before Silver, the Lone Ranger's favorite steed, was Hobb E. Horse. Even fewer people know that the Lone Ranger began his illustrious career rescuing teddy bears in distress. (Photograph © J. C. Allen & Son)*

OUR BEST CHRISTMAS

By Clarence Hill

Clarence Hill, a farmer from western Iowa, shared the following heartwarming Christmas memory with readers of *Farm Journal* in the magazine's December 1953 issue.

A shaggy, pot-bellied little Shetland pony got all mixed up with our Christmas last year. I'd like to tell you about it.

Our four boys are in the pony business; you'll see that from our sign along the road, which reads: "Kids love ponies; ponies love kids."

Ponies, like children, have personalities. Major Midget, our chestnut stallion, 38 inches tall, 14 years old, is a gentleman in the hands of Eleanor, 7, but with our four boys he is full of tricks, devilish, and unpredictable.

About a dozen Shetland foals are born on our farm each year. "First to see a colt gets to name it," we say, and the result is a lexicon of names, such as Dagwood, Scamp, Cheffy, and Twinkle.

Then Sparkle came along. A proven brood-mare, she was also the gentlest pony we ever owned. Jet black, she had that comfy look, with a broad and matronly middle, like Mom and Aunt Esther when they're not cinched up for Sunday.

In our six-pony hitch, Sparkle was literally our anchor mare. She couldn't be hurried.

The village kids adored her, and loaded her up with humanity on the outside, and with apple cores inside.

Sparkle had horse sense. She would stand motionless while a child got out from under her chassis, but she likewise kicked the daylights, as well as the tail-lights, out of a boy who annoyed her colt.

One of the unwritten codes of our business is that no one shall become so attached to any pony, sentimentally, that it may not be sold. But already Sparkle had become an exception. She just wasn't for sale!

It was the week before Christmas that the Baxters came—a tired-looking father and a very-very-red-headed little boy of seven. Billy Baxter's eyes were so blue, and his freckles so unanimous, that you hardly saw the limp that polio had left him with.

We learned, in four words, why Mamma hadn't come along: "His mother is dead."

The doctor had said that Billy needed some incentive to exercise. A pony might be just the thing—might become a playmate, too, to make his life less lonely.

Here was one order we couldn't fill. We didn't have any pony that was that safe—none, that is, except old Sparkle, who wasn't for sale.

But between boy and beast, it was love at first sight—a silent communication between black mare, with her long whiskers and warm nose, and red-headed boy with eager, tense face.

Would we price the mare? The twins Ed and Art (16) were noncommittal. Robert (12) and Harold (10) objected. Eleanor rebelled. So we called a conference.

Could Sparkle, even in a small way, help heal the lame leg? The doctor had said yes.

But most important, could this decision become our greatest gift this Christmas—not something easy, but a genuine sacrifice of something loved?

We delivered old Sparkle on Christmas Eve. Bob and Harold went along, across the Des Moines River and over near Polk City. I was sorry we arrived at dusk, for a motherless farmstead is loneliest when night, and Christmas Eve, come on.

But a light was in the barn. We found a clean stall with fresh bedding and bright hay, and a red-headed boy.

It was then that I knew what I wanted for Christmas tomorrow: just ten sturdy legs and ten strong arms for my five children and Mother Mabel to be waiting at dusk each day.

Something was happening to Robert and Harold, something as great and as timeless as Christmas itself. They were sensing their own participation in the fulfillment of another's dream. For now, Billy had four more legs to help him, and a friend to roam the pasture with when spring came around.

"Sometimes . . . great lessons are taught in stables."
—Clarence Hill (Photograph © Marilyn "Angel" Wynn)

The freckle-faced boy stood—wordless—watching the pony, and I wondered if her barny-smell and loose dandruff weren't frankincense and myrrh to him.

We left Sparkle then, my two boys and I. We didn't have much to say as we rode home, but deep inside us, I know we shared something: a strange warm glow, warm enough to melt my eyes just a little.

Sometimes, I thought, great lessons are best taught in stables.

At the Des Moines River bridge we slowed down awhile, and looked back at the Baxter barn where one star sparkled down—bigger, more brilliant, and warmer by far than all the others. At least, that's what the two little wise men said who sat beside me in the truck.

The Year We Had No Christmas Tree

By Ben Logan

In writing his memoir *The Land Remembers: The Story of a Farm and Its People*, Ben Logan's goal was "to record a time and place of great value that had gone uncelebrated." The time was his childhood in the 1920s and 1930s and the place was Seldom Seen, a farm set in the rolling hills of southwestern Wisconsin. His record is a finely detailed account of a pastoral way of life in days gone by, laced with a quiet affection for the family of that family farm.

Although his careers as a United States Navy midshipman, magazine editor, television and film producer, and teacher took him from New York to Mexico, his roots remained planted in the land of Wisconsin. Eventually, that land called him back; he returned to the farm of his youth in 1986 and still resides there today.

In the following chapter from *The Land Remembers* (1975), Logan reminisces about the nature of his family's holiday celebrations on the farm, but recalls that one Christmas that occupies a special branch at the top of his glittering tree of holiday memories.

Come out and play
In farm country, the "perfect powder" lays right outside the front door, just waiting for the tramp of a snowshoe, the glide of a ski, or the rush of the sled. (Photograph © Daniel Dempster)

EVEN WHEN I was very young, Christmas was a time of memory. It stretched back across the years, filled with all the kaleidoscopic rememberings of other Christmases, always moving us close together in a special time of loving and being loved. It reached back even beyond my own birth. I could see earlier Christmases in the way Mother hung a favorite, faded ornament on the tree, in the way Father's face softened when he began to sing a Christmas carol in Norwegian. Always one of my brothers would say, "Remember the time the dog knocked the tree down?" I couldn't remember, but I could see it. It became so much a part of Christmas that one year I beat everyone else and said it myself. No one realized that I only remembered through their remembering.

There was a tinseled star at the top of the tree, always speaking of ancient times and three wise men, reminding me of Father traveling across the wide sea, guided home by stars, lighthouses, and, now, by Mother's lamp burning in the kitchen window.

Christmas was, and is, lights and colors, warmth and laughter, remembered voices and all the sad and happy sounds of childhood. It is the feel of heavy brown wrapping paper, the tune of a music box with a bright yellow knob, the smell of pine pitch and of an orange being peeled. It is the first flash of the incredibly red dump truck I got when I was seven years old, the buttery smell of sugar cookies, the feel of the finely worked wool of a new turtle-neck sweater that no older brother had ever worn. It is the silvery tinkling sound of a candy wrapper as I unveiled a mysterious chocolate, then put the smoothed-out foil into an encyclopedia along with the faded flowers and bright candy wrappers from other years.

Christmas was a season within a season, filled with mystery and wonder. How could it be such a part of us, yet still seem to come from outside ourselves? How could it be new each year, yet always be the same Christmas, the way it is with an old and familiar tree that is always there, yet always has new growth?

I don't know the answers. I only know that each year we reached out to find Christmas and make it happen, and each year Christmas reached out and found us instead. It found us even in that strange winter we always spoke of as "the time we didn't have a Christmas tree."

The season began as usual. The last day of school came, and that was the first day of Christmas for us.

Teacher, as always on that day, had a frantic look. We could not stay in our seats or keep from whispering.

"Let's meet! Let's go sledding!"

"When?"

"Tomorrow! Day after tomorrow! Next week!"

"Let's each say we're going to stay at the other's house. We'll dig a snow cave. We'll sled all night."

"If there's a wet snow, let's all come back to school. Let's start a big snowball. Let's roll it down the hill until it's big as the schoolhouse. "

"Yeah, and maybe knock the schoolhouse down!"

We squirmed in our seats, and we weren't even there. We were racing up and down the hills on our sleds, defying gravity, snow flying up to pelt us, giving us faces so white that only our eyes showed through, and the adults fainted and screamed when they saw us, thinking we were ghosts.

All Teacher could think of was the school program that night. We were her performers, and we couldn't even remember our own names.

"Quiet. Get back to your seats. Stop that whispering."

We stayed an extra half hour to practice the singing. Teacher couldn't seem to get us all to use the same words. For "Jingle Bells" was it "Bells on bob tail ring," or was it "Bells on bob-tailed Ned" (or "Nag" or "Nob")?

"You've got me so confused I don't remember myself," Teacher said. "Let's agree it's Ned."

We tried another song. "No! No! It's 'We Three Kings of Orient Are,' not 'We Three Kings of Oriental.' And when you're singing 'Silent Night,' remember that it's 'round yon virgin,' not 'round, young virgin.'"

"Can you all remember that?"

"Yes," we cried, the feel of our sled ropes already in our hands. We would have said yes if she'd asked if we each had thirty-nine heads.

A first-grade girl had to stay after school for more work with Teacher. She had decided to recite the Lord's Prayer and she kept saying, "Our Father Who are in Heaven, Halloween be Thy name."

We ran for home, pulling our sleds, still making plans.

"Let's build a ski jump!"

"Let's pour water all over the hillside west of the house and slide on the frozen crust."

We had used water once to make an icy crust on

Snow play
Two Indiana girls celebrate Christmas by taking their doll and sled outside to play in the snow. (Photograph © J. C. Allen & Son)

Oh boy, fresh snow!

In creating her paintings, Sandi Wickersham's goal is to tickle the viewers' fancies and spark nostalgic feelings. "There is so much humor and whimsy everywhere we look, if we only let the child in us come out and see it!" she says. (Artwork © Sandi Wickersham)

Sledding school
*Unfortunately, one can't be outside sled-ding all the time. (Photograph ©
Ronald H. Wilson)*

the big snowdrift between the house and barn. Father and Lyle didn't know about that. They started across the drift carrying a ten-gallon can full of milk. It was a good crust all right. After Father and Lyle fell down, they stayed on top and slid all the way down to the chicken house. When the milk can caught up with them, it still had enough in it to slosh them good. Father suggested we not do that any more. He also suggested we spend the next day shoveling a path through the big snowdrift.

But a whole hillside of ice would be different! We'd go flying down toward the fence, skim under the lower strand of barbed wire, teeter on the edge of the ditch, and go all the way to the woods!

Junior wasn't there to ask things like how would we get the water out there and what if we hit a bump just as we went under the barbed wire. He was at home with a cough. When we came crashing into the kitchen, Father and Mother were talking about whether or not Junior should go to the school program that night. Junior was looking from one to the other as they talked, his face pale, eyes very big. He smiled when they decided it would be all right.

We did the chores before supper. Lyle finished the last half of his hot coffee in one noisy gulp and hurried out to get the horses and the big bobsled ready. With the yellow light of a lantern to show us the way, we went out to the sled. Lyle had filled the two-foot-high sled box with straw and put all our old blankets on top. Mother had heated several of her irons on

top of the kitchen stove and brought them along, wrapped in old towels, in case anyone's feet got cold.

We blew out the lantern and climbed in, pulling blankets around us. Lyle was up front. He flipped the lines, said, "Gid-y-ep," and we glided out along the ridge to the west, the wind reaching for us, the tug chains ringing like bells behind the trotting horses.

Our eyes adjusted to the darkness. A faint blue light seemed to hang just over the surface of the snow. We could see the graceful roll of the drifts along the road, the smooth outline of snow-covered fields, the faint shadow of the next ridge to the north and beyond that the lights of Mount Sterling.

Father was wearing his old horsehair coat and had promised Mother he would leave it in the sled. Mother's hands were tucked deep into her big fur muff, holding it up to protect her face from the wind. Junior was huddled almost out of sight in Father's big sheepskin coat. The sled runners rattled sometimes when we hit crusted snow.

"Look!" Mother said, pointing.

There were glittering little pinpoints of light shining in a field where the wind had swept away the snow and uncovered patches of smooth ice.

"What are they?"

"The reflection of the stars," said Father.

We lay down on our backs, protected from the wind, sinking deep into the straw with its smell of summer, and we looked up at the distant stars.

"How many do you think there are?"

"A billion, I bet."

"A trillion."

"Eighty-nine thousand quadrillion."

"So many you could spend the rest of your life counting them and still not count them all."

"Is it always the same stars?"

"Of course it is."

"I mean if you tried to count them, would they all just stay there and be the same ones?"

"Hey, maybe there's stars that just visit us, maybe once every thousand years."

"Comets do that, not stars."

"Well, why shouldn't a star be able to do that if a comet can?"

"Shush," said Mother. "Just enjoy them."

We went on into the shelter of the woods. The wind was almost gone, the breath of the horses quick and white as they walked up the steep hill beyond the deep ravine. We topped the hill and turned down into the narrow school road, sled runners gliding silently through the undisturbed snow, bare limbs of trees so thick above us they almost shut out the stars. An owl hooted. Something quick and small, a rabbit maybe, scurried away from the road and vanished in the woods.

"There's the light," Lyle said as we came down into the little hollow that led to the schoolhouse. The runners of other sleds were rattling on the icy road beyond the creek. Horses were whinnying. Yellow lights bobbed up and down in the meadow east of the schoolhouse where people were coming on foot, carrying kerosene lanterns. We found a place between two other teams, tied up to the top rail of the fence, and Father and Lyle covered the horses with blankets.

The schoolhouse was warm, filled with the light and smell of a half dozen kerosene lamps. One was flickering. Mother smiled at me. "It needs you to trim the wick."

The big wreath we had made from pine limbs and bittersweet berries was hanging under the clock. The blackboard had hundreds of little dabs of chalk on it.

"I told you it wouldn't look like snow," Junior said when he saw the blackboard. His voice was a hoarse whisper. He stayed with Mother in a front seat, his hands tucked inside her muff. Soon the room was crowded, some people dressed "in their best bib and tucker," as Mother would say, some in work clothes

Show stopper

The best country school Christmas pageants, including those of cartoonist Bob Artley's youth, aren't Broadway-caliber shows. But what they lack in production, they make up for in heart. (Artwork © Bob Artley)

that carried a barn smell through the warm room. There was a burst of laughter when a long-legged man tried to squeeze into the desk he'd used when he was in the eighth grade.

"Look," he said pointing at the desk top, "there's my initials."

Several high-school boys stood at the back of the room, whispering and laughing. A girl near them got up, marched to the front, and crowded into another seat, her face as red as the ribbon in her hair.

Teacher welcomed everyone. Mostly she talked about how hard we had worked. I think she was asking people not to laugh at our mistakes.

We all trooped out of the cloakroom for our first number, jostled into position, and sang "Jingle Bells," almost everyone remembering to say "Bells on bobtailed Ned."

Steepled church in winter
Like many of today's holiday cards, turn-of-the-century holiday postcards featured country scenes. This German-made postcard from the early 1900s depicts a steepled church in winter.

The next number was "Scenes from an Early Wisconsin Christmas." The piano began. An Indian crept out, an arrow ready in his half-drawn bow. When his head feather slipped, he grabbed for it and the arrow went up in the air and came down on the piano keyboard, playing one sharp pinging note. The woman at the piano, I think her name was Elsie, slid over to the other end of the bench. It tipped and dumped her off. She reached up and went right on playing while she was getting up from the floor.

Tom Withers came in, crawling on all fours, playing a hungry bear. The Indian was supposed to shoot him, but he couldn't find his arrow. Tom ran in circles, one of them carrying him too close to the Christmas tree. His head went through a loop in a string of popcorn. Tom kept on going. The tree tipped and came down on top of him. He roared, as a bear or as himself we never knew, and galloped off with the string of popcorn following.

The audience did its best. People were able to control their laughter until a boy came out for the first lines of our scene.

"Christmas in early Wisconsin," he said, "was not an easy time."

"By God, you can say that again," boomed a voice from the back. "What with bears in the house and all."

The room filled with laughter. Men were pounding their legs and wiping tears out of their eyes. The women stopped first and began shushing everyone until it was quiet again.

A third-grader marched out to do her piece about Christmas fairies. After four sentences or so, she forgot her lines and switched over and did "The Village Blacksmith" instead. The audience applauded anyway and she walked off, head high, looking very pleased.

A boy did part of "Snowbound." I don't think he understood the opening lines because he always put a question mark after them. "The sun that cold December day, it sank from sight before it set?"

A girl began reciting "The First Snowfall." Halfway through, her little brother wandered up front and stood looking up at her. She went on speaking, shooing him away with her hands, but he stayed right beside her. She stopped for a minute, sighed, then took his hand and went on with the poem, the little boy beaming at her. There was a line in that poem about someone kissing a child, then lines something like

WHEN 'TWELVE DAYS OF CHRISTMAS' WASN'T VERY PROMISING

Being sick

Being sick is never fun, but being sick over Christmas vacation just isn't fair, as Bob Artley remembers in this panel. (Artwork © Bob Artley)

"And she kissing back could not know that the kiss was meant for her sister, lying deep under the falling snow."

The girl took the little boy back to his seat and walked to the cloakroom. The audience was very quiet, except that one old lady in a white shawl was crying. Then the applause came, longer for that girl than for any other part of the program.

We all lined up and started singing "Joy to the World," but were interrupted by the sound of horses fighting. Half the men ran outside, and we waited, frozen in the middle of a line, until everyone came back. The piano started again at the beginning. We went on from where we were. At the end, an angel was supposed to walk across in front of us. One of her wings fell off. She tripped on it and said, in a clear whisper, "Darn! I told her it wouldn't stay on."

Everything else went all right unless you counted a key sticking on the piano and a man prying it up with his jackknife.

At the end, we all jostled into line again and sang "Silent Night." I don't think we said the virgin was round. The old lady started crying again. Teacher

walked out in front of us and said, "Everybody sing!"

The whole schoolhouse rumbled and vibrated as all the voices joined in.

We waited for the applause to end, bowed, and started to walk off, but there was a cold blast of air from the door and Santa Claus bounced in with a big bag on his shoulder. He went ho-hoing around the room, stopping every few steps to pull up his slipping belly, asking who had been good all year in a voice suspiciously like that of one of our closest neighbors, Amel Oppreicht. He came up to the front, reached into his bag, and handed each of us a little brown paper sack full of hard candy, peanuts, and a big sticky popcorn ball that stuck in the top of the sack like a bottle stopper.

Santa went all around the room with little sacks for the younger children and for Junior, pretending each time that his bag was empty. Then he bounced back out the door. We could hear him yelling out in the schoolyard. "Gid-y-ep, Dancer! Gid-y-ep, Prancer!"

We crowded to the windows. He was riding off in a sled. Bells were ringing, and he yelled, "Merry Christmas to all, and to all a goodnight! "

The sled, the voice, and the bells faded slowly into the night.

The piano started up again. Everyone crowded around to sing carols, and the smell of the kerosene stove filled the room as women began making coffee and hot cocoa. Soon it was ready, great steaming pots of both, along with about a hundred different kinds of cookies that were shaped like stars, trees, and bells, most of them covered with bright-colored sugar.

Warm, and so full of cocoa we could hear it sloshing when we wiggled our stomachs, we started home. Lanterns were going in all directions, the night filled with young and old voices.

"Merry Christmas!"

"Goodnight. Merry Christmas."

"See you in two weeks."

"Don't forget we're going to roll a big snowball."

We went up the road, Denny Meagher and his sister, Margaret, close behind us in their sled. We said "goodnight" and "Merry Christmas" to them, then turned out along Seldom Seen ridge by ourselves. The moon had come up. The trees made sharp black shadows on the snow. Mother began singing "Oh, Little Town of Bethlehem," her voice high and clear, getting lost out against the bright stars. Father's deep voice joined her, his Norwegian accent more noticeable when he was singing. We all sang, except Junior, as the horses trotted toward home.

We got out in front of the house and Lyle took the horses on to the barn. Junior was coughing, looking very white when Father carried him inside.

"Open the davenport," Mother said to Lee and me.

The davenport was in the living room. We opened it and Father put Junior down, then carried coals from the dining-room stove for a fire. Sticky from the popcorn balls and still working on the hard candy and peanuts, we went off to bed with two weeks of vacation ahead and plans enough to fill a year.

Junior was still sick next day and the day after that. The door to the living room stayed closed except when we tiptoed in to put more wood on the stove.

Dr. Farrell came from Seneca, bundled up in a big coat and a fur cap, riding in a little sleigh that we called a cutter. We ran out to take his horse.

"I'll give her some water and oats," Lyle said.

"You will, will you?" Dr. Farrell roared. He had a voice, Lyle liked to say, that was like a cream can full of walnuts rolling down a steep hill. The doctor headed for the house with his bag, then yelled over his shoulder, "By God, it's a help all right, having the horse taken care of."

We watched from the dining room doorway while he warmed his stethoscope over the stove and listened to Junior's throat and chest. He left the thermometer in for a long time "Cause it's cold as a damned icicle to start with!" When he read the thermometer, he came out into the dining room, closing the door behind him. Father and Mother were waiting.

"Scarlet fever," Dr. Farrell said.

"What does that mean?"

"Means he's going to be a mighty sick boy. Keep the other children out of that room. Be better if only one of you goes in there." He went on talking to Mother while we got his horse and hitched it to the cutter.

Junior kept getting worse, his fever so high we could hear him mumbling and talking in his sleep even with the door closed. Once he said in a loud, angry voice, "I said I wanted skis!"

It was a strange Christmas season. We didn't do any of the things we'd planned. Mother hardly had time to talk to us, except to tell us what needed to be done. Dr. Farrell came every day. Then, maybe four or five days before Christmas, Mother told us there wouldn't be a Christmas tree

"We'll do something about it later, maybe. There just isn't enough time now. Anyway, the doctor says we have to keep the house quiet." She was almost crying when she went into the other room and closed the door.

"You help her all you can," Father said. "Don't wait to be asked."

"Is Junior going to get well?"

He looked at us for a long time. I used to wonder when he did that if he was thinking in Norwegian and had to change it back to English.

"We don't know," he said.

I don't remember how Laurance felt about what was happening, but Lee and I began to feel cheated.

Roll out the carol

Natural talent isn't enough to make you the star of a Christmas Eve program. Getting to the top requires lots of practice at home and a few rehearsals for Mom and Dad. (Photograph © J. C. Allen & Son)

Winter wonderland
A New England orchard awakens frosty and glittering after an overnight ice storm. (Photograph © Paul Rezendes)

In the safe isolation of the big dark closet at the head of the stairs, we dared to come right out and tell each other there wasn't any Santa Claus. I'm sure we already knew it wasn't Santa who brought our presents, but he had gone on being a part of Christmas for a long time and we still believed in Christmas, all right. But what kind of a Santa Claus, even if he was just a "spirit," would let Junior get this sick at Christmastime?

We still ran to meet the mailman every day, hoping for packages, especially packages with revealing rattles or holes in them. One day George Holliday handed us one that didn't need a hole. He winked and laughed. "Here you are. What comes in a package four inches wide, five feet long, and curves up at one end?"

"Junior's new skis," we said.

"How is he?"

"Still sick."

"Well, when he gets his skis, he'll be better."

"He won't be getting them. We don't even have a Christmas tree."

"Well hell's bells," George said. "No wonder he's sick."

We took the skis to the house and gave them to Mother. She put them away. "He might not even know if I gave them to him."

Lee and I spent more and more time in the dark closet, trying to get Christmas to happen. All our other Christmases began to form in our minds as we talked. We always cut two or three branches from the white pines in the yard and tied them together to make a nice full tree. We hung all the ornaments, some of the tin ones old and dented. We put up the star and threaded popcorn and cranberries onto strings and draped them around the tree. There was a little package that unfolded and magically became a big red paper bell to hang over the dining-room table, so low we had to be careful not to put the lamp under it. On Christmas Eve we always turned the lamp down low and lighted the candles on the tree, Father watching from the kitchen door with a bucket of water in his hand. We would look at the burning candles and eat the little round candies with pictures in the center that were a promise of what was to come in the morning.

Christmas Day always began with the presents, but there was much more. Father would put out his sheaf of grain for the birds. There were navel oranges and bright red apples that made our own seem pale and small, and always a letter from Norway with a strange stamp, the envelope lined in brightly colored tissue paper. We'd all sit down and Father would tell us what the letter said, giving us a once-a-year glimpse of a grandmother and aunts and uncles who were only pictures in the old leather suitcase.

Soon, the smells of Christmas dinner would spread through the house, so strong and good we forgot our presents and gathered, starving, in the kitchen to hurry Mother along. Father said a blessing in Norwegian and we ate until we couldn't hold another bite, then ran around the table four times and ate some more.

After dinner Mother would bring out the package of books. Each year, just before Christmas, she sent off a letter to the State Lending Library, asking them to send us about thirty books for three adults and four boys. She gave our ages and a few words about each of us. She'd never let us read what she said, though sometimes she'd include our suggested additions, things like "Please don't send Black Beauty again this year." Then someone in the library in far-off Madison would read the letter and would, we liked to think, sit down, close their eyes, see us, and decide what books to send.

Only then, with everyone gathered in the warm house, with presents, books to read, and all the good things to eat, would Christmas have really come.

Lee and I could go back over all that in the closet, but this time it didn't happen. We ran into the dining room on Christmas morning and it was just like any other day, except that Mother looked sad and hollow-eyed and Father was walking restlessly around the room. Dr. Farrell came right after breakfast. We heard him say something about "today being a critical day."

When the doctor left, Mother brought out a present for each of us. They weren't wrapped with the usual bows and ribbons. I guess Father must have done them. Lee and I got the double-barreled popguns we'd been wanting. Wondering how we could have missed a package that slim and long, we tore them out of the boxes, cocked them, and started to pull the double triggers. Father grabbed us.

"Better go outdoors with those."

We went out and tried target practice for a while, using twigs, corks, and pieces of ice for bullets. It began to snow, big wet flakes. We rolled giant snowballs, leaving paths of bare brown lawn behind us, and made a snowman, then used our new popguns to shoot

The mail's here!

At no other time of the year is the mail carrier's visit so eagerly anticipated. December deliveries bring holiday greetings and letters from friends and family far away, catalogs full of gift ideas, and packages filled with cookies and other Christmas treats. (Photograph © Marilyn "Angel" Wynn)

marbles into his front for buttons.

It didn't feel like Christmas, even with the snow falling. We sat down with our backs against the snowman and waited for something to happen.

What happened was that a man we'd never seen before came walking along the road from the west. He was wearing a stocking cap and had a stick over his shoulder with a little bundle on the end. Sometimes tramps came by with a bundle like that, heading for the railroad along the Kickapoo River. The man saw us sitting there against the snowman and waved to us.

"Merry Christmas!" he called in a big voice.

We waved back, and he went on walking down the road with the snow falling around him.

We started talking about Junior and Christmas again. The first thing we decided was that Junior should get his skis. But we had to do more than that.

"We could say Santa Claus came by with them."

That wasn't going to be good enough for skeptical Junior.

"What if somebody did come by? And saw us sitting here?"

"Yeah, somebody like an old man with a stocking cap and a bundle on his back."

"What if he asked how come we weren't happy

and playing?"

"Yeah, and we said because our brother's sick."

"And maybe he'd be like Mr. Holliday. He'd say, 'No wonder he's sick. What you need to do is take him his present.'"

"And tell him he's going to be all right."

"Do you think he'd believe that?"

"Maybe the old man better have a beard."

"Yes, a red beard."

Dr. Farrell stopped by again and we followed him into the house. He came back out of the other room and said, "He's no better."

"Can we see him?" Lee asked.

Mother shook her head.

"We want to give him his skis."

Mother looked at Dr. Farrell. He sighed. "Oh, it can't hurt anything. But don't go up close. Stay away from the bed."

Mother got the skis. We unwrapped them and took them in, closing the door behind us. Junior was lying on his back, two pillows under his head. His eyes were open but he didn't look at us. He was making a funny noise when he breathed, and his freckles stood out very plain. He didn't even seem like Junior.

We held up the skis so he could see them. We started telling him about the old man.

Pretty soon Junior looked at us. When he started shaking his head a little bit, it was Junior all right.

"Tramp," he whispered.

"No, it wasn't! He had a long beard."

"A red one!"

Junior stopped shaking his head and seemed to be thinking about that. We shoved the skis onto the bed and pushed them up beside him. He took a deep breath and closed his eyes.

We tiptoed out.

"Did you give him the skis?"

"Yes. And he went to sleep."

Mother started for the other room. Dr. Farrell stopped her. He went in and closed the door. When he came out he looked surprised. "That's right. He is asleep. I think he's breathing better."

Mother hugged us. For the first time it seemed like Christmas.

Four or five days later, when Dr. Farrell came by, he said Junior could get up the next day. Mother smiled and said she thought maybe she'd go to bed when he got up. She looked at us. "I'm sorry about the tree."

"Hummp!" said Dr. Farrell. "Seems to me Christmas came anyway!"

Merry Christmas, Elsie!
Above: *Legend says that on the night Jesus was born, all the animals in the stable were given the ability to speak, so that they could rejoice in his birth. Many farm families remember that story today by hanging wreaths on their barns.* (Photograph © Lynn Stone)

Full moon
Overleaf: *A full moon rises over the mountain to shine on a lone Christmas tree.* (Photograph © William Johnson)

"After this has been digested thoughtfully the reader may wander through the pages of the book just as he might wander over the farm if he wished to learn something of country life."
— Peter McArthur, *In Pastures Green*

Finishing touches
*A towheaded youngster puts the finishing touches on his holiday decorations.
(Photograph © J. C. Allen & Son)*

Permissions

Text

"Township Christmas" by Justin Isherwood. Reprinted from *Christmas: An Annual of Christmas Literature and Art, Volume 55* © 1985 Augsburg Publishing House. Used with permission from Augsburg Fortress.

"The Spirit of Christmas" from *Chips Off the Ol' Block* © 1997 by Bob Becker. Reprinted with permission from the author.

"The Taste of Country Christmas" from *The Taste of Country Cooking* © 1976 by Edna Lewis. Reprinted by permission of Alfred A. Knopf, Inc.

"Christmas at Thornhill Farm" from *Hollyhocks, Lambs and Other Passions* © 1985 by Dee Hardie. Reprinted with the permission of Scribner, a Division of Simon & Schuster.

"Oh, Tannenbaum!" from *All My Meadows* © 1977 by Patricia Penton Leimbach. Reprinted with permission from the author.

"Notes from a Christmas Tree Grower" © 1993 Beverly Shaver. Originally printed in *Country Journal* magazine, November/December 1993. Used with permission from the author.

"To the Farm and Back" from *An Old-Fashioned Christmas* © 1964 by Paul Engle. Used with permission from Hualing Engle.

"A Green Gables Christmas" by L. M. Montgomery. Reprinted from *Anne of Windy Poplars* © 1936 by L. M. Montgomery and used with the authorization of David Macdonald and Ruth Macdonald, heirs of L. M. Montgomery. *Anne of Green Gables* is a registered trademark and a Canadian official mark of the Anne of Green Gables Licensing Authority, which is owned by Heirs of L. M. Montgomery and the Province of Prince Edward Island and located in Charlottetown, Prince Edward Island.

"Recipe for Christmas" from *Mainstays of Maine* © 1944 by Robert P. T. Coffin. Used with permission from the estate of Robert P. T. Coffin.

"Toys from Dad's Workshop" by Bob Artley. Reprinted from *Christmas: An Annual of Christmas Literature and Art, Volume 59* © 1989 Augsburg Publishing House. Used with permission from Augsburg Fortress.

"Our Best Christmas" by Clarence S. Hill. Originally printed in *Farm Journal* magazine, December 1953. Used with permission from *Farm Journal*.

"The Year We Had No Christmas Tree" from *The Land Remembers* © 1975 by Ben T. Logan. Reprinted by permission of Frances Collin, Literary Agent.

Artwork

"Twilight Glow" and "Sleigh Bells, Too" © 1999 by Bill Breedon. Exclusively represented by Applejack Licensing International. Used with permission from Applejack Licensing International.

"Not the Same Old Grind," "It's Starting to Look a Lot Like Christmas," "Dog Days of Winter," "Winter Memories," and "Oh Boy! Fresh Snow" © Sandi Wickersham. Used with permission from the artist.

Cartoons from *Memories of a Former Kid* © 1978 by Bob Artley and *Cartoons: From the Newspaper Series "Memories of a Former Kid"* © 1981 by Bob Artley. Used with permission from the artist.